RAISE YOUR
VOICE

Also by Jeffrey Kluger

TO THE MOON!

DISASTER STRIKES!

RAISE YOUR VOICE

VOICE

JEFFREY KLUGER

12 PROTESTS
THAT HELPED SHAPE
AMERICA

PHILOMEL

PHILOMEL

An imprint of Penguin Random House LLC, New York

First published in the United States of America by Philomel,
an imprint of Penguin Random House LLC, 2020
First paperback edition published 2024

Visit us online at PenguinRandomHouse.com.

The Library of Congress has cataloged the hardcover edition as follows:
Names: Kluger, Jeffrey, author.
Title: Raise your voice : 12 protests that shaped America / Jeffrey Kluger.
Description: New York : Philomel, 2020. | Includes index. | Audience: Ages: 8–12 |
Audience: Grades: 4–6 | Summary: "A recounting of protests throughout American history
that have shaped our nation"—Provided by publisher. Identifiers: LCCN 2019030850 (print) |
LCCN 2019030851 (ebook) | ISBN 9780525518303 (hardcover) | ISBN 9780525518310 (epub)
Subjects: LCSH: Demonstrations—United States—History—Juvenile literature. | Protest
movements—United States—History—Juvenile literature. | Political participation—
United States—History—Juvenile literature. | United States—History—Juvenile
literature. Classification: LCC HN57 .K565 2020 (print) | LCC HN57 (ebook) | DDC
303.48/40973—dc23 LC record available at https://lccn.loc.gov/2019030850
LC ebook record available at https://lccn.loc.gov/2019030851

ISBN 9780525518327

1st Printing

Printed in the United States of America

LSCC

Edited by Jill Santopolo. • Design by Ellice M. Lee.
Text set in Baskerville Std.

This is a work of nonfiction. Some names and identifying details have been changed.

To all those who
have stood up
and spoken out

TABLE OF CONTENTS

INTRODUCTION

YOU CAUGHT AN awfully lucky break when you were born a person. We all did. There's a lot for humanity to be proud of, after all. We're the species that mastered art, that mastered science, that understands geometry and biology and astronomy and medicine. We build rockets and send spacecraft to other planets; we design buildings that tower half a mile into the sky; we dig tunnels underground where we accelerate subatomic particles nearly to the speed of light and use them to crack open the secrets of the universe.

We are, too, the species that knows how to love. Other animals surely bond deeply and powerfully to one another. They protect their babies; they guard their herds and flocks and packs. Elephants, dolphins and crows mourn their dead, bury their remains and caress their bones. Yet we are the species that feels and celebrates love in all its dimensions and all its depths. We would give our lives for the life of another—because to live without a loved one sometimes seems not to be alive at all.

And yet, we can be terrible too. We are the species that mechanized war, that commits murder out of rage or greed, that betrays friends or families if it means accumulating wealth. Worst of all, perhaps, we separate ourselves into camps: we divide ourselves by race, by gender, by religion, by nation, by sexual orientation, by politics and class. And it is the more powerful group that often exploits the less powerful.

Men claim rights they deny to women; white people claim privileges they have forbidden to Black people and other people of color. Owners of companies cheat their workers; political groups with power exploit those without. Industrialized countries pollute the planet, indifferent to the needs of less industrialized ones. Heterosexual people drive gay people into the shadows. Nations with empires oppress their colonies. Countries with nuclear weapons terrorize the entire world.

We know better; indeed, we're hardwired to know better. Scientists who study the mind have looked at which parts of the brain become active when we witness something that's fundamentally unfair—a person cheating at a game, a landlord raising a rent so high that an elderly person is tossed into the street, a drug company charging so much for a medicine that sick people can't afford it. The region of the brain that becomes active when we witness such things turns out to be the same region that goes to work when we feel disgust. It is, in some ways, an admirable part of us: we react to the thought of unfairness in the same way we do to the smell of a rotten egg or the sight of spoiled meat.

And yet if we're disgusted by unfairness, we don't always act that way. Down through the millennia, strong and dominant groups have again and again worked their will against weaker and subordinate ones. But down through those same ages too, the disadvantaged and the oppressed have risen up. Emperor Caligula was overthrown in ancient Rome. The Jewish slaves in ancient Egypt cast off the pharaoh's yoke. The oppressed Black people in South Africa took back their rights from the oppressing whites. The imprisoned nations of Eastern Europe wrenched themselves free of the old Soviet Union.

The United States itself was born in an act of rebellion, with the thirteen colonies rearing up against the king of England. Throughout our relatively brief history, that liberation tale has been told again and again, with Black people and women and poor people and more recognizing injustice—recoiling from it as a thing turned foul—and demanding the freedoms that are their right. It's an act not just of rising up, but of speaking out—and, when necessary, crying out.

Americans have raised their voices many such times over the centuries, and no one group's liberation story is greater than any other's. The ongoing battles for the right to live where you choose, to love whom you love, to have the job you want and the social freedoms you deserve, to vote for the people who will make the laws and vote against them if you don't like those laws are all a part of our shared history.

And the best part of that—the part that activates the regions of the brain that light up at the thought of something sweet or just or good—is that when one group becomes freer, so do we all. The twelve stories of civil uprisings that follow are by no means the only ones that have shaped America, but they are among the ones that have shaped us most—and they are ones that teach us lessons still.

The Boston Tea Party, as re-created by an artist in 1846.

ONE

The Boston Tea Party
1773

IT WASN'T EASY to tell the difference between the bad guys and the good guys if you lived in Boston in 1773. A few of them, of course, were hard to mistake. The British soldiers were certainly bad guys—at least the way the colonists saw them. It was the soldiers, after all, who strode about in their military finery and enforced the laws that came from a king who lived across the ocean in a land almost no one in Boston had ever visited. That by itself made it hard to understand why such a man should be able to tell the colonists what to do, but never mind, he did.

The king told them what kinds of laws they could pass and what kinds they couldn't; how they were to conduct trade with the rest of the world and how they were not. He set the prices of their goods and controlled their local governments and decided the taxes that they'd have to pay. And he could stop them from gathering in meeting houses or public squares to debate all of those problems if he chose. The soldiers made sure the rules were obeyed, and if the colonists objected, well, the guns the soldiers carried and the warships in the harbor would soon change their minds. So the soldiers were certainly the bad guys.

The lieutenant governor of Massachusetts had seemed like a good guy once. He had a pleasant enough name—Thomas Hutchinson. And he had a pleasant enough appearance—slight, owlish and harmless-looking. He was from Great Britain, but he admired the colonies and made himself a scholar of colonial history. But back in 1765, he had begun working hard to enforce the taxes the British were imposing on the colonies. The worst of them was the so-called Stamp Act, which required the colonists to buy and use only official English paper, marked with a telltale stamp, to print their newspapers, magazines, legal documents and even playing cards. Though this was one tax Hutchinson opposed, by then he was seen by the colonists—correctly—as one more agent of their oppression and so they attacked his mansion and destroyed much of his artwork. After that, the colonists and their lieutenant governor didn't really get along.

But there were a lot of other prominent people in Boston, and it wasn't always easy to tell whose side they were on or what they were up to. That made it awfully difficult for the British to figure them out—and the prominent people liked it fine that way. There was Thomas Young, a well-respected writer and physician who was so wise in the ways of medicine that, even in 1764, he had begun working on the idea of battling smallpox by developing something known as a "vaccine," which could prevent people from ever contracting the disease. Few people had heard of such a thing, but Young was convinced it could work.

There was Samuel Adams, a political philosopher and newspaper publisher, who came from a line of beer-makers and dabbled in the family business too. There was no doubt that Adams was civic-minded—concerned with the welfare of Boston under the rule of England—but it was unclear whether so reflective and intellectual a man could pose much trouble. There were less prominent people as well, like George Hewes, who worked as a shoemaker and was just the kind of person no British soldier would ever take much notice of—as long as he obeyed the king's laws and paid the king's taxes. There were plenty of other Bostonians like him: industrious, orderly, obedient. Indeed, of the 17,000 people living in the young colonial city, most—if by no means all—could be counted upon to behave themselves.

That was partly why the soldiers did not give much thought to the reports that mentioned that sometime in September, four ships would be heading out of England and would eventually arrive in Boston, carrying cargo that included a total of 340 cases—or 90,000 pounds—of tea. Bostonians loved their tea, a habit they had picked up from the British themselves, and they would surely be pleased at its arrival. It was unlikely that so prized a cargo could ever lead to trouble.

If Great Britain wanted to maintain the peace with its colonies in America, it had never quite acted that way. As early as 1651, the kingdom drafted and imposed what were known as the Navigation Acts—taxing all the trade the colonists could conduct with the rest of the world. Workers and shippers in America would undertake the hard work of growing crops or mining ore or cutting timber, then embark on long and perilous journeys to export it all around the world, and when they were done, the king would help himself to a bit of what they had earned. If they complained, he would close their ports altogether. In 1673 came the Plantation Duty Act, which specifically taxed tobacco and sugar and sent revenue collectors to the colonies to make sure the taxes got paid. In 1764 came the Sugar Act, which taxed those and other commodities more strictly, ensuring that the taxes were collected and that merchants couldn't avoid them; in 1765 came the hated Stamp Act, and in 1767 came the Townshend Acts, which taxed glass, lead, paint, paper and, finally, tea. For the first time, the British had touched the colonists' beloved tea.

The way the colonists saw things, it wasn't so much the taxes themselves that were the cause for outrage. It was the way they were imposed. Like nearly all established nations, Great Britain had a constitution. Unlike the people in most established nations, however, the British never wrote theirs down. Their constitution was, instead, a series of rules and practices and long-standing traditions; committed to paper or not, its principles were honored. One of the *most* honored of them was that while taxes are necessary for any government to run, the people would never be made to pay them unless they were represented by members of Parliament who would be looking out for their interests and—it was hoped—vote only for taxes that were fair.

But the colonists had no representatives in the British Parliament. They did not have a vote, they did not have a voice, and yet they were taxed—and, it felt to them, taxed and taxed and taxed. It was, as the phrasing went, "taxation without representation," and the colonies were fed up with it.

Over time, they began to push back, led by a secret organization known as the Sons of Liberty, which included Boston's Samuel Adams; the Virginian orator Patrick Henry; the New York tailor and American spy Hercules Mulligan; the Philadelphia physician and social reformer Benjamin Rush; and many more across all thirteen colonies. They led protests, they distributed political leaflets, they smuggled the goods the British were taxing and sometimes they boycotted them—denying themselves sugar or tobacco, putting off buying needed lead or paint. The British couldn't collect taxes, after all, on goods that no one buys.

In 1770, on a cold and snowy day in early March, blood was at last shed, when a confrontation between resentful colonists and a group of soldiers guarding the headquarters of the British colonial government on King Street in Boston escalated to taunting, which escalated to shoving, which escalated to spitting and snowball throwing. Eventually, someone threw a rock or other heavy object, which struck British private Hugh Montgomery in the side of the head, causing him to fall and drop his gun. He recovered it and struggled to his feet.

"Fire!" he shouted to the other soldiers.

And so they did fire, striking eleven colonists and killing five of them—including a seventeen-year-old boy named Samuel Maverick, who was an apprentice learning to make elegant objects like chess pieces, tobacco pipes and parts of musical instruments out of soft wood, ivory and ebony. Maverick was standing at the back of the crowd— likely just to watch—and was hit by a musket ball that ricocheted off of something in its path before it reached him.

The bloodshed on King Street was quickly dubbed the Boston Massacre, and both sides knew something had changed that day—a deadly corner had been turned. The king responded badly. He continued his oppressive laws, not only taxing the colonies without their consent, but dissolving their local governments, occupying their very homes with soldiers, denying them trial by jury. Even before Great Britain learned of the Boston Massacre, Parliament, in a small concession, had repealed the Townshend Acts. But perhaps as an insult—a sort of finger in the eye of the disobedient colonists—the tax on tea was retained. In May 1773, an additional tea tax, straightforwardly called the Tea Act, was also imposed. That final act—one more bit of royal spite—would prove to be too much.

It wasn't until the summer that the colonists learned of the new tax, and it was later still, in early fall, that they would learn that a flotilla of seven ships loaded with tea had set sail from England. One each was heading for Philadelphia, New York City and Charleston, South Carolina. Four were headed for Boston.

In Philadelphia, Benjamin Rush urged the colonists to reject the tea, warning that in it lay the "seeds of Slavery." But the Philadelphia ship had no way of knowing this, so it landed in the city anyway, as did the one in New York and the one in Charleston. One of the Boston-bound ships, the *William*, ran into a storm and arrived in port seventy miles to the southeast, in Cape Cod. The sailors unloaded the tea—before the locals had time to reject it—climbed back aboard and headed back to England.

The first of the ships to reach Boston, the *Dartmouth*, arrived on November 28. There was no way of knowing if the ship's captain, James Hall, saw the handbill that was circulated around Boston on the morning of the twenty-ninth. But if he did, he surely realized that he had sailed right into a world of trouble.

"Friends! Brethren! Countrymen!" it began. "That worst of plagues—the detested tea—is now arrived in the harbor. The hour of destruction, or manly opposition to the machinations of tyranny, stares you in the face."

The second ship, the *Eleanor*, landed on December 2. The third, the *Beaver*, arrived last, on December 15. They all sat anchored at busy Griffin's Wharf, under the hateful gaze of the Bostonians, who would have been happy to pay a fair price for the tea, but not if an unfair tax was attached. Even without a local government under their own control to tell the Bostonians how to respond to the arrival of the boats, there was citywide agreement that the tea must not be unloaded. All along the pier, more than two dozen men affiliated with the Sons of Liberty stood guard, making it clear by their presence alone that the ships' crews would have a fight on their hands if they didn't leave the tea exactly where it was, stowed in the ships' holds.

In New York, Charleston and Philadelphia, where the resentment was equally great, the public acted fast, with demonstrations and declarations calling for the ships to leave and take their tea with them; in Philadelphia especially, there were mass protests. It was the British East India Company that processed and owned the tea that was being shipped to the colonies, and the company typically hired colonial merchants to act as what was known as consignees—people who would take possession of the tea as it was unloaded and then sell it to local merchants. Ordinarily, to be a consignee of a product like tea was a fine and profitable job. You didn't have to do the hard work of the planting or picking or shipping; you just managed the sales and collected your pay. But in New York, Charleston and Philadelphia, that was suddenly dangerous work and all the consignees resigned. The Philadelphia and New York ships turned around and headed back to England with their tea, as the colonists demanded. In Charleston, the tea was unloaded and held by consignees, but then seized by local officials who stored it in a warehouse and would not allow it to be sold. That ship too then went home.

But in Boston, Lieutenant Governor Hutchinson would not tolerate such disobedience. Even if the consignees resigned, he would find other merchants to do their work; if none stepped forward, his own officials would take over the job. No matter what, the tea would be sold, the tax would be paid and the three ships would not leave the harbor until every one of their collective 340 chests of tea had been unloaded. To make that point as vividly as possible, British warships were anchored at the mouth of the harbor, making it impossible for the commercial ships to leave until they'd been unloaded.

At first, there was no trouble. All three ships were carrying other cargo besides the tea, and all of that was peacefully unloaded. But mobs of Bostonians at Griffin's Wharf were watching, and if so much as a single chest of tea touched the pier, there would likely have been riots. Nobody—British or American—wanted another Boston Massacre.

On the morning of December 16, the local leaders of the Sons of Liberty organized a mass gathering in Boston's Old South Meeting House, on the corner of Milk and Washington Streets, to discuss what to do next. Two thousand people filled the hall and the grounds outside; seven thousand others gathered in the streets. The decision was made that a peaceful resolution would be attempted first. The owner of the *Dartmouth*, Joseph Rotch, who owned a fleet of merchant ships and really wanted nothing more than to sail them in peace, would be sent to visit Lieutenant Governor Hutchinson at his home in Milton, Massachusetts, and ask for permission to sail home, since all the cargo save the tea had been unloaded. If the *Dartmouth* were allowed to leave, the *Eleanor* and the *Beaver* would probably be free to follow.

The lieutenant governor's home was ten miles away from the meeting house, and Rotch was given only until 3:00 p.m. to travel there, secure permission and return. It was not a realistic deadline, but neither was it realistic to think that Hutchinson would grant his permission. Still, decorum and, even then, a sense of fair play dictated that a last chance be offered. The Sons of Liberty and the others in the hall, meantime, had already planned what their next move would be.

By 3:00 p.m., Rotch had not returned and the mood in the meeting house grew surly, though the people there and in the streets agreed to wait a bit longer. Shortly after sunset, which came early, at 4:16 p.m., on that December day, Rotch did return. Hutchinson, as predicted, had said no.

Shouting broke out among the people inside, but Samuel Adams rose and cut through it all.

"This meeting," he declared, "can do no more to save the country."

History would never quite agree on whether Adams's words were a signal to begin what came next or simply a lament that captured the frustration and anger that everyone else in the hall was feeling. Whichever it was, events unfolded fast. A roar erupted from the crowd, and one more voice—according to the accounts that would be passed down over the generations—cried out, "Boston Harbor a teapot tonight! Hurrah for Griffin's Wharf."

At that, the people in the hall swarmed for the exits and several dozen of them—an estimated sixty men and boys—set about executing the plan they had decided upon: disguising themselves in various ways, grabbing weapons and making their way to the three ships under the direction of three group leaders.

Sixty was a manageable number for the event that was planned, but with hundreds, perhaps thousands, of others following them and hundreds more down at the wharf already, the mob would surely grow out of control. Inside the hall, Thomas Young, the patriot doctor, rose and called for attention. The crowd inside, which had not yet been able to reach the exits, turned as Young announced that he had an important matter of public health to discuss. In wintertime—when colds, bronchitis and pneumonia could sicken and kill—a public health address from the likes of Dr. Young was something that deserved attention, even on a night like tonight. The doctor, however, did not rise to speak about colds or bronchitis or pneumonia. He rose to speak about the terrible risk posed to public health by drinking tea.

It was a clever bit of misdirection—one that was not quite delivered with a smile and a wink, but might as well have been. The king's tea, the doctor told the crowd, was close to poison. Even if the British soldiers still somehow forced it to be unloaded, there would be fewer people lining up to buy it now. Either way, the crowd stayed and listened—and that kept them off the streets.

As Young spoke, the sixty attackers continued their advance on the wharf. Most of them had chosen to disguise themselves as members of the Mohawk tribe of Native Americans, a signal to the British that they felt they too had become native to the new continent. Hewes, the Boston shoemaker, was one of the attackers. He and a small group of other men hurriedly pulled on Mohawk-like garments they had carried with them, ducked into a blacksmith's shop and smeared their faces with coal dust from the smith's stove, hoping to conceal their identities. Then, brandishing small tomahawks, larger axes and clubs, they arrived at the wharf. As crowds of Bostonians watched, they followed the direction of one of the three leaders, who pointed the arrivals onto each of the three boats. Most of the attackers took no notice of the name of the boat they were ordered to board; all of them carried the hated tea in equal amounts, so it mattered little.

Once aboard, Hewes took the lead and made his way to the captain's cabin, demanding the keys to the hold where the tea was kept, as well as candles so that his men could find their way. The captain knew that there was nothing he or the few other crewmen aboard could do against twenty armed men. His true responsibility was not to his cargo, which changed every voyage, but to the great vessel that had been entrusted to him. He handed over the keys and candles on the condition that the attackers would leave the ship unharmed; Hewes promised they would—and that promise was kept.

On the other two ships, similar scenes played out: for some of the attackers the work was quiet and even grim; for others it was thrilling. Joshua Wyeth, a boy of just sixteen, had heard whispers of the plan to attack the tea just a few hours before it was to begin. He hastily assembled a costume and lurked out of sight near the meeting hall until the crowd began moving to the wharf. He then blended with them unnoticed and scanned the faces of the bystanders happily, searching for people he recognized and delighting in the fact that they did not recognize him in return. When he reached the wharf, the group he was part of boarded a different ship from Hewes and made similar demands of and promises to the crewmen: if the crew unlocked the hatch and provided them with the rope and pulleys to lift out the 114 tea chests, no harm would come to them or their vessel. The crew agreed, and Wyeth and the others leapt into the hold.

"We were merry in an undertone at the idea of making so large a cup of tea for the fishes," he would recall to historians many years later. "But we used not more words than were absolutely necessary. I never worked harder in my life."

Women and girls, as was the way of things in the eighteenth-century world, were not allowed to participate in the events at the wharf directly, but they helped as they could. One group of rebels included Nathaniel Bradlee, a Boston craftsman. He and a handful of others gathered first at the home of his sister Sarah, who helped them with their disguises and was credited as the person who suggested that dressing as Mohawks would carry a powerful meaning that the British might or might not understand, but that the rebels themselves would. In appreciation of her contribution, many people of the time would come to refer to her as the Mother of the Boston Tea Party.

Aboard all three of the ships, the work progressed methodically—and exhaustingly. Each of the 340 chests of tea was heavy and all of them had to be wrestled up to the deck. They were all wrapped in heavy canvas and rather than taking the time to remove that first, then try to open the lids and get at the tea, the attackers simply began hacking at the canvas and the thick wood beneath with their axes and tomahawks. The more holes they chopped, the more water would saturate—and destroy—the tea when the chests were thrown overboard.

A great deal of loose tea was scattered about on the decks as the chests were chopped and tossed into the harbor, and a few Bostonians, who had gone a long time without fresh tea, scrambled onto the ships to grab what they could. At least one rebel on each vessel was given the job of stopping the thefts; Bostonians were in this together, they agreed—a unified city within a unified colony—and they would suffer without their tea together too.

A respected military man known throughout town merely as Captain O'Connor was one of the attempted thieves, but Hewes spotted him as he was scooping up tea leaves and stuffing them into his coat pockets. He lunged for O'Connor as he was trying to leave the boat, caught him by the bottom of his coat and pulled it off him just before he leapt down to the dock. The people on the ground saw what had happened and administered more than a few kicks to O'Connor as he ran through them and made his escape. A tall elderly man with a stylish hat and a white wig that was fashionable for men at the time stole some tea too—and was spotted as well. The crowd snatched his hat and wig and tossed them in the water—along with the tea he had stuffed into his pockets—but given his age, they spared him most of the kicks O'Connor had suffered.

Finally, after three hours of heavy, loud labor, all the tea chests had been hacked open and thrown into the harbor. By prior agreement, the rebels then hurried down the ships' ladders onto the dock, cleaned up the remaining tea that had been scattered there and tossed it into the water. Then they melted into the crowd, discarding their costumes in alleyways or trash bins along the way.

"We quietly retired to our separate residences, without having any conversation with each other," Hewes recalled much later in life. "Nor do I recollect of our having had the knowledge of the name of a single individual concerned in that affair. There appeared to be an understanding that each individual should volunteer his services, keep his own secret and risk the consequence for himself."

The sun rose on a cold and quiet Boston on the morning of December 17. A few of the rebels who had been on the boats the night before made their way back down to Griffin's Wharf to check for stray tea that might still be stolen and sold. There was none on the dock, but there was much floating on the water. Spying unattended rowboats tied to the dock, they hopped aboard, rowed out to the floating tea and beat it with oars until it sank. Then they disappeared again.

It would take a while for reports on the revolt to reach England—news could travel only as fast as boats could sail. The king thus did not learn of it until January and, even then, found it hard to believe that the colonists—*his* colonists—would be capable of such treachery. But by March, letters from Hutchinson and from one of the consignees who had been appointed to take possession of the tea confirmed that the rebellion had indeed occurred. When the king informed his government of what had happened, the reaction was furious. In Parliament, the prime minister, Lord North, thundered, "They ought to have their town knocked about their ears." He condemned the colonies as a whole, but saved particular venom for Boston, which he called "the ringleader in every riot."

Parliament agreed and swiftly passed a series of laws the colonists dubbed the Intolerable Acts, which included shutting down the port of Boston and disbanding all local government bodies, stripping the entire Massachusetts colony of the power of self-government. Even some patriots and rebels who opposed the Intolerable Acts were uneasy with what the Bostonians had done. Benjamin Franklin, the celebrated newspaper publisher, writer, scientist and political philosopher, argued that the Boston colonists should at least pay for the tea they had destroyed, which, at two British shillings per pound, came to £9,000—or $1.8 million in modern American currency.

But Franklin—who would go on to become recognized as one of America's founding fathers—was in the minority in the days following the tea party. John Adams, who would become the second president of the United States, captured the national mood—and the change the tea party had wrought in the colonial mind—much better. On the morning after the tea was dumped, he wrote in his diary: "This is the most magnificent movement of all. There is a dignity, a majesty, a sublimity, in this last effort of the patriots . . . This destruction of the tea is so bold, so daring, so firm, intrepid and inflexible, and it must have so important consequences . . ."

And it did. Word of what Boston had done spread through the colonies fast—leading to more resistance and more defiance among the 2.5 million people who were increasingly coming to think of themselves not as British citizens, but as Americans.

On April 19, 1775, fighting broke out between British soldiers and militiamen in the towns of Lexington and Concord, both in Massachusetts—the first shots in what would become known as the Revolutionary War. On July 4, 1776, the Declaration of Independence—formally declaring that the United States had separated from Great Britain and stood alone as a free nation—was signed. Six years of fighting would follow, costing 25,000 American soldiers their lives; an equal number of British soldiers were killed. The blood that was spilled on the battlefield, historians would come to agree, flowed in a long and rushing stream from the tea that was spilled in Boston harbor on a cold night in December 1773. The deaths were a terrible price; but it was a price that, over time, would produce a great nation.

Elizabeth Cady Stanton's home in Seneca Falls, New York.

TWO

The Seneca Falls Convention
1848

THE CROWD WAS huge in front of Exeter Hall in London on the morning of June 12, 1840. At least 1,500 people would be swarming inside as soon as the doors opened, with perhaps more to follow. About 500 of them would be serving as official delegates for the important meeting that would be taking place inside; the other 1,000 would be spectators—and there would be plenty to see when the debates began. With so many people being welcomed into the hall, it was a keen disappointment when the two American women presented themselves at the door and were told that they were not welcome inside, at least not the way they had come here expecting to be.

The two Americans had had a hard time getting to London at all. It could take six weeks to cross the Atlantic Ocean by sail—a bit less if you had favorable winds, more if you did not. Either way, the North Atlantic was a nasty stretch of water and getting from one side of it to the other could mean a lot of discomfort and a lot of seasickness—and a lot of boredom. Still, it was worth the effort, because the two women and the 1,500 others who were descending on Exeter Hall had come for a very good reason: to abolish the blight that was slavery.

The United Kingdom was proud of its opposition to the horrific practice of buying and selling human beings as if they were cattle or lumber or crops, especially because the practice was based on race. It was the light-skinned people of Europe who were the owners, and the dark-skinned people of Africa who were the slaves, and untold millions had suffered and died in bondage as a result of so savage a practice. But the fact was, the U.K. had only recently come to oppose slavery officially, having abolished it on almost all land under its authority just seven years earlier, in 1833. Still, that put it ahead of much of the rest of the world where slavery was still practiced, including parts of Russia, the Caribbean, the Ottoman Empire, South America and most notoriously the United States, where nearly 2.5 million Black people were held against their will.

A global problem that huge called for a global solution, and so it was a very good thing when Joseph Sturge, a British businessman who practiced the Quaker religion, called for an international convention to discuss ways to abolish slavery forever. The idea was taken up by William Lloyd Garrison, a celebrated anti-slavery crusader in Boston, who owned a newspaper called the *Liberator* and who published an article in 1839 proposing just such a convention. Anti-slavery—or abolitionist—groups around the world rallied to the idea, and an eleven-day convention was planned for the very next June.

The world's abolitionist organizations had the authority to select the people who would represent their countries as delegates, and they were careful to choose the most passionate and persuasive of their members. For the abolitionist groups in the United States, those delegates included Lucretia Mott and Elizabeth Cady.

Cady, just twenty-five years old, was born in Johnstown, New York, one of eleven children—five of whom died in childhood. One more brother, Eleazar, died at age twenty, when Cady herself was just eleven. In a family with so much hardship, Cady was determined to help in any way she could, but there was only so much she was allowed to do. After Eleazar died, she tried to comfort her father, assuring him that she would be able to fill in for her lost brother, achieving all the things he might have achieved and helping to look after her surviving siblings as well. Her father's response stung her.

"Oh, my daughter," he said, "I wish you were a boy!"

All the same, Cady persisted. Her father was an attorney and her mother was the daughter of an officer who had fought in the American Revolution, and while they may not have understood the potential in their daughter, they did encourage her to get an education, enrolling her in the nearby Johnstown Academy. She was just sixteen when she graduated and applied straightaway to Union College, which Eleazar had attended. But Union rejected her, in keeping with their policy of accepting only boys, so Cady enrolled instead at Troy Female Seminary in Troy, New York.

She studied hard at Troy and excelled at her work—especially her writing, which was elegant and powerful. In her free time, she also worked with her father to learn the law, paying special attention to the way it enforced the dominant position men held in in the world and the subordinate position of women.

In 1840, she married Henry Stanton, a journalist, attorney and committed abolitionist, but only on certain conditions. Marriage vows traditionally included the bride's promise that she would "love, honor and obey" her husband, and while there was nothing wrong with the love-and-honor part since it was something that husband and wife owed each other equally, she refused to promise obedience, and her new husband agreed. She also insisted that while she would take her husband's surname, Stanton, she would not drop her own, Cady. She would be known by both or she would not be wed. He agreed to that too. The newlyweds were in complete agreement from the start on the abolitionist cause and worked hard in its service. When Cady Stanton was selected by her local group to attend the convention in London, she and her husband thus decided to have their honeymoon there so they could combine their vacation and Elizabeth's work.

Mott came from a world that was both similar and very dissimilar. A Quaker like Sturge, she was born Lucretia Coffin, on Nantucket Island in Massachusetts, and attended Nine Partners School, a Quaker School in eastern New York State. She graduated and became a teacher there, and she met and married another teacher named James Mott. She enjoyed her work but could not help but notice that the pay of all of the women at the school was much lower than that of all of the men, which seemed unfair but was simply the way of things.

Ultimately, Mott's family moved from Nantucket to Philadelphia and Lucretia and James moved there as well, but she didn't stay put. In addition to her work as a teacher, she was also a minister, a position that in the Quaker religion was open to both men and women. That was a very good job for Mott because it turned out she was a brilliant, compelling speaker. One thing she spoke out about most was slavery, which a portion of the Quaker religion first formally denounced in the seventeenth century. In 1833, Mott cofounded the Philadelphia Female Anti-Slavery Society. By 1840, she was an obvious choice to attend the London meeting.

That obvious choice, however, turned out not to be a welcome choice for the organizers of the convention. When Mott and Cady Stanton and the other women chosen as delegates arrived at Exeter Hall, they were told that they would not be permitted to serve in their assigned roles. It was just not fitting for women to participate in politics— at least not publicly. All of them would instead be assigned to a seating area off the main floor, where they could hear the proceedings but not be part of them. A few men objected to that arrangement, among them Garrison, who refused to take his place among the other male delegates and instead sat with the women. It was wrong—absurd even—that in a convention intended to advance human rights, anyone would be excluded on the simple basis of sex.

Sometime over the course of those twelve days, Mott and Cady Stanton met and began chatting, sharing their ideas about justice and liberty and a woman's place in the world. They decided that place should be a large and powerful one—every bit the equal of the place men inhabited. And they decided that they would help make that happen.

"As Mrs. Mott and I walked home arm in arm, commenting on the incidents of the day," Cady Stanton would later recall, "we resolved to hold a convention as soon as we returned home, and to form a society to advocate the rights of women." They were not the kinds of people to break such a pledge.

It would be eight years before Elizabeth Cady Stanton and Lucretia Mott could start to set the world to rights, but in the meantime, there were a lot of injustices that they and other women would have to continue to tolerate. It wasn't just that women could not vote or sign contracts or buy land. It wasn't just that they couldn't establish credit or take out loans or go to the schools that they chose. It wasn't even that they were forbidden to take most jobs, limited instead to service positions like childcare or secretarial work or teaching, all of which are perfectly fine—often wonderful—professions, except that if you were a woman who didn't *like* childcare or teaching or secretarial work, well, that was just too bad.

Perhaps worst of all was the subordinate role women had in their own marriages. Cady Stanton may have refused to promise to obey her husband and he may have agreed with that, but there were plenty of laws that discriminated against women that they could not change. Any property that a woman brought into a marriage would become the property of her husband. The same was true of any property she acquired during the marriage. If her husband died, creditors could take her property to pay his debts. In the event that the couple divorced, the custody of the children often went to the father without the mother even having a chance to argue her case.

Still, Mott knew that for the time being at least, it was slavery that was the leading condition social reformers like herself were working to change, and she directed her efforts there, traveling the country speaking out for abolition. It was an exhausting business—and it could be a dangerous one too. Mott visited not only Northern states, where slavery had been outlawed already, but slave-owning states, including Virginia and Maryland.

Cady Stanton also campaigned against slavery, as well as in favor of temperance—the prohibition of alcohol or at least the strict limitation of its sale and use. In some ways, she believed, this was very much a woman's issue too, since women were expected to limit their drinking strictly while men were not, and if a woman married a man who had trouble controlling his alcohol—who became angry or violent when he was drunk—divorce laws made it difficult for her to leave the marriage. If she reported his abuse to the police, they would often shrug, saying it was a private matter between the husband and wife.

By now, Cady Stanton and her husband had moved to Boston, where he worked in a law firm and she had the chance to get to know Garrison better, as well as to meet and mingle with Frederick Douglass—a former slave and one of the leaders of the abolitionist movement—and Louisa May Alcott and Ralph Waldo Emerson, both writers. Her conversations with them fired her zeal for women's rights, and in 1842, when Mott visited Boston, she and Cady Stanton spent time together and spoke again of their commitment to do for other women what the abolitionist movement was doing for slaves. In 1847, Cady Stanton's husband's health began suffering as a result of the frigid, sooty Boston winters, and they decided to move to Seneca Falls, New York, where the winters were still bitterly cold, but the air was cleaner and the breezes fresher.

Seneca Falls was a good—even lucky—choice, because in the summer of 1848, Lucretia Mott and her husband happened to be passing through. They were in the area to visit the Native Americans of the Seneca reservation, wanting to learn more about the gender equality practiced by the local tribes. They were also planning to stop by a community of former slaves—who had likely escaped bondage and fled the country—living across the nearby Canadian border in Ontario. And, of course, Mott wanted to spend time with her good friend Cady Stanton.

On July 9, the two of them got together for tea with three other women: Mary M'Clintock, a Quaker like Mott and a friend from Philadelphia who now lived just to the east in Auburn, New York; Martha Coffin Wright, Mott's sister and an active abolitionist, who lived just to the west in Waterloo, New York; and Jane Hunt, a relative of M'Clintock, who also lived in Waterloo. The tea was held in Hunt's home.

During the course of the long afternoon, the group took to discussing women's rights, and Cady Stanton later recalled that the other four were attentive as she shared "the torrent of [her] long-accumulated discontent." They had not had quite the same experiences she had, since she did not belong to the Quaker religion and they did, and were thus part of a community that strove for equality between men and women.

But that community was part of a larger world in which women were treated as very much *un*equal.

As the five of them discussed that fact, they decided together that enough was at long last enough. They could not change the world by themselves, but they could start. What was needed, they decided, was precisely the kind of convention Cady Stanton and Mott had discussed in London eight years earlier. It might not be as big as the anti-slavery gathering at Exeter Hall, and it certainly would not be in as grand a city. But it would happen soon—immediately, almost, while Mott was still in town—and it would happen nearby, in Seneca Falls, at the red-brick Wesleyan Chapel, a sensible, comfortable space that could hold at least a few hundred delegates.

There is one powerful thing that can stop people who are planning such a bold and even dangerous thing from actually doing it—and that is the passage of time. Let enough hours or days pass, and the risks of even a very good idea like a women's rights convention can start to present themselves: no one would pay attention to them; worse, people would pay attention and would laugh at them; the women would get in trouble with the police or their families would be shamed. So at that moment, around that very tea table, the five women in Jane Hunt's parlor drafted a notice that they would immediately send to the *Seneca County Courier.*

"WOMAN'S RIGHTS CONVENTION," the announcement read. "A convention to discuss the social, civil, and religious condition and rights of women." The notice, which would also be printed on leaflets that could be distributed by hand, set the date for the two-day meeting at just a week and a half away—July 19 to 20. On July 11, the announcement appeared in the paper and the women knew there was no turning back.

Over the course of the next week, they gathered again to decide on the agenda for the convention. The women would be declaring their freedom—just as the American colonies had declared their freedom from Great Britain seventy-two years earlier. And so they would borrow the language of the Declaration of Independence itself—but they would call their document the Declaration of Sentiments, and they would change the text in critical ways.

"When in the course of human events, it becomes necessary for one people to dissolve the political bands which have connected them with another . . ." the Declaration of Independence began.

"When in the course of human events, it becomes necessary for one portion of the family of man to assume among the people of the earth a position different from that which they have hitherto occupied . . ." the Declaration of Sentiments answered.

"We hold these truths to be self-evident, that all men are created equal . . ." the Declaration of Independence stated forthrightly.

"We hold these truths to be self-evident: that all men and women are created equal . . ." the Declaration of Sentiments rightly amended.

And both documents would lay their accusations directly at the feet of their oppressors:

"The history of the present King of Great Britain is a history of repeated injuries and usurpations, all having in direct object the establishment of an absolute Tyranny over these States . . ." is how the colonists framed their accusation.

"The history of mankind is a history of repeated injuries and usurpation on the part of man toward woman, having in direct object the establishment of an absolute tyranny over her . . ." is how the Seneca Falls women framed theirs.

Like the colonists who drafted the Declaration of Independence, the women who drafted the Declaration of Sentiments listed the evidence for their accusation. And then, unlike the colonists, they drafted a second document, a list of eleven resolutions—proposed changes in laws and customs that would ensure equality between the sexes. The resolutions demanded that women be allowed to work in any field in which a man works, that they should be free to speak publicly and to participate fully in religious practice as teachers and congregation leaders, that all laws that accord women second-class status—including marital laws—should be overturned, that women should be allowed to vote. Less formal customs could not be done away with by legal action, but the eleven resolutions demanded that they change too: women who performed in plays or dance halls or circuses, for example, were often looked down upon, particularly by men, as if they were unworthy of participating in polite society and certainly would not make good wives—and yet it was mostly the men who came to see them perform. Similarly, men who had many romances were widely admired for their popularity with women, while women who had many romances were told to be ashamed. Both sexes, the women demanded, should be judged by the same standards.

Of all the eleven resolutions, it was the ninth—the one that concerned voting rights—that the five women around the tea table knew would be the most controversial. Many men, even Cady Stanton's own husband, thought that it was asking too much—that while women might be equal in all other spheres, it was still the men's job to choose the nation's leaders. No surprise, those men almost always chose other men. But the women included the resolution anyway. They were either to be men's equals or they were not—and if they were, then they should vote.

Cady Stanton, Mott and the other three had one additional matter to decide upon: Should men be allowed to attend their convention? It was the men who had oppressed them for so long, after all; what business would they have being part of the effort to topple that oppression? The colonists did not invite King George's representatives to be part of their legislatures or sign their Declaration of Independence, did they?

But the Seneca Falls women decided that yes, men would be invited to attend. The women were setting an example of a society that valued both sexes equally. Besides, their goals would be better achieved if the men could be made to see why they were just and proper. There would, however, be one limitation on the men: they could attend only on the second day of the meeting; the first day the women would have the gallery to themselves.

That day, July 19, dawned a sweltering one, with the thermometer reaching a high of ninety degrees Fahrenheit. Despite that, close to 300 women packed into the little chapel, sensing they just might be making history. Cady Stanton spoke first, addressing the assembly with a 3,000-word speech that took more than forty minutes to deliver. Her words were as blistering as the temperature:

"Among the many important questions which have been brought before the public, there is none that more vitally affects the whole human family than that which is technically called Women's Rights," she said. "Every allusion to the degraded and inferior position occupied by women all over the world has been met by scorn and abuse." But that scorn, she argued, which typically came from men, should be ignored because "woman alone can understand the height, the depth, the length, and the breadth of her own degradation. Man cannot speak for her."

Mott addressed the assembly too, as did her sister Martha. The Declaration of Sentiments was read aloud, along with the eleven resolutions, and they were all debated. Each of the resolutions would be voted on separately and each would stand or fall on its own. It was decided that all the attending women would be allowed to sign the final document, but no one would be required to, in case they wanted to keep their presence there a secret. The women debated whether the men who attended the next day would also be allowed to sign, and adjourned for the evening without a decision.

The second day of the meeting, the resolutions were read and debated again, and several dozen men did attend—including Frederick Douglass, who addressed the convention. Unlike the other men in the room—who were elevated by law on the basis of nothing more than their color and their gender—Douglass could understand what oppression felt like, by virtue of the years he spent in slavery, as well as the bigotry and oppression he still experienced as a free Black man. He kept his remarks brief, mindful that this was the women's day and that he had the power only to advise, not to decide. But he was proud to do that small bit, and a full forty years later, at an event commemorating the Seneca Falls meeting, he reflected on that pride.

"When I ran away from slavery, it was for myself," he said. "When I advocated emancipation, it was for my people; but when I stood up for the rights of woman, self was out of the question, and I found a little nobility in the act."

Douglass spoke powerfully, movingly, but in some ways, his very presence there exposed a hole in the planning and the very purpose of the convention. He was the only Black person in the room. The initial handbill announcing the convention did not explicitly exclude Black women; it certainly did not specify that the gathering was for white women only. But in 1848—nearly a generation before slavery was abolished in the United States—the assumption was always that such public gatherings were whites-only events. If Black people were going to be admitted—and they virtually never were—that would have to be stated clearly.

Mott and Cady Stanton—abolitionists both—surely understood

that if all women were disadvantaged in a world dominated by men, Black women were doubly so, once by their gender and again by the color of their skin. That the doors of the convention were not flung open to women of all races and colors may have represented a lapse in Mott's and Cady Stanton's thinking—a racial shortsightedness that they themselves might have been ashamed to acknowledge. Or it might have been tactical: when you're fighting for justice, you don't always try to right all wrongs at once, lest you wind up righting none at all. Rather, you fix the problems you can and hope, with that greater power, that you can go on to fight another day for other kinds of justice.

If the Seneca Falls gathering would leave some kinds of injustice unaddressed, however, it would still achieve great things when, on July 20, 1848, the women in attendance adopted and published their Declaration of Sentiments in full. The eleven resolutions all passed—ten of them unanimously, with only the one concerning voting rights receiving any dissenting votes. Men, it was decided, would be permitted to sign the final pronouncements, but in a separate part of the document. Sixty-eight women signed, as did thirty-two men. For all one hundred, it was an act of courage.

When stories about the Seneca Falls meeting began to appear in newspapers in the days to follow and the Declaration of Sentiments and eleven resolutions were published and read, the response was uneven. Horace Greeley, the powerful editor of the *New-York Tribune*, whose newspaper did a great deal to help shape public opinion, grumbled about the voting rights resolution but had to admit that it was hard to argue with anything the women had decided.

If a sincere American were asked, he said, "what adequate reason he can give for refusing the demand of women to be in equal participation with men in political rights, he must answer, None at all."

The *Daily Reveille*, a St. Louis newspaper, went further, declaring that "the flag of liberty has been hoisted for the second time on this side of the Atlantic."

But other newspapers heaped scorn on what the Seneca Falls women had done. "This is all wrong," read a commentary in one Albany paper, the *Mechanic's Advocate*. "Society itself would have to be radically remodeled in order to accommodate itself to so great a change."

The Philadelphia *Public Ledger* openly sneered: "A woman is nobody. A wife is everything. A pretty girl is equal to ten thousand men."

But the sneering would amount to nothing; the disdain would have to fall away—or if it didn't, it would have to be stripped away. Just as the signatories of the Declaration of Independence knew they would have to fight a long war before Great Britain would accept colonial independence, so too did the women of Seneca Falls know that their daughters and granddaughters and great-granddaughters would have a generations-long struggle ahead of them.

The struggle would be a difficult but successful one: laws would change, but slowly, state by state and sometimes community by community. Colleges would open up to girls and women, as would fields of employment and politics, but here too every step would be a fight. It would not be until 1920—seventy-two years after Seneca Falls— that the Nineteenth Amendment to the Constitution would be ratified, giving women the vote. It would not be until 1984 that a woman would be nominated for vice president of the United States by a major political party and not until 2016 that a woman would be a major party's presidential nominee. Challenges remain: women may have achieved equal access to education and career choices—including the military and space exploration—but they still must fight to earn the same incomes men earn. More women may be part of the U.S. Senate and House of Representatives than ever before—but men still make up nearly 80 percent of the total.

All the same, if history has shown anything, it's that once the great wheel of justice has begun to turn, it does not stop turning until equality, decency and freedom are achieved. For women and girls in the United States, that wheel began to move over the course of two sweltering days in upstate New York in 1848. It is moving still.

Garment workers march in memory of the lives lost at the Triangle Shirtwaist Factory.

THREE

The Triangle Shirtwaist Factory Fire and the Fight for Workers' Rights
1911

IF YOU WANTED to get up from your sewing machine in the Triangle Shirtwaist Factory in New York City, it was a good idea to turn sideways as soon as you stood and sort of shimmy along, as if you were leaving your seat in a movie theater. There were a lot of other girls crowding over a lot of other sewing machines on the top three floors of the ten-story office building known as the Asch Building, off of Washington Square Park, near New York University. It was best not to count how many girls there were, and most of the girls didn't have time anyway, which was how it was when you worked close to seventy hours a week—more than twelve hours a day, Monday through Friday, plus eight extra hours on Saturday for about two-thirds of the employees. The long days might be regrettable, but the owners of the factory—Max Blanck and Isaac Harris—believed they were necessary if the company was going to manufacture enough of the fashionable, flouncy blouses known as shirtwaists that their customers liked to buy in fine stores all over the city.

If you were employed by Mr. Blanck and Mr. Harris, it was smart to pay close attention to your work. Damage one of the garments you were making and some of your wages would be held back to pay for it—and there wasn't much of that pay to begin with. If you were what was known as a "learner," you'd earn perhaps three to four dollars a day—minus any amount that would be deducted from your paycheck not just for a damaged blouse, but as a penalty if you ever showed up late.

You could make more—seven to twelve dollars a day—if you qualified as an operator, but somehow Mr. Blanck and Mr. Harris were never quite satisfied with the work the girls did, and so did not see any cause to award them the promotion. The operator jobs generally went to the few men who worked for Triangle. They were surely more qualified than the girls, the owners concluded, and they were certainly more experienced.

On that score—the experience—the owners were right, but mostly just because of the age of the girls. Some were in their twenties, but many more were in their teens—a few as young as fourteen. The majority of them were immigrants—belonging to Jewish families from Eastern Europe and Russia. There were also Germans, Italians and Hungarians. The girls might have objected to their low pay and long hours, but as their bosses reminded them and reminded them and reminded them, they were lucky to have any work in the first place.

If so, an awful lot of them had gotten lucky that way. There were about 240 workers on each of the three floors, or 720 in all, seated at eight long tables of 30 workers each—15 to a side. There was very little space in the aisles between the tables; lean back even a bit on your bench and you'd hit the back of the girl behind you. That was the reason for the sideways walking if you needed to get up from your work for any reason—not that you had much opportunity to do that either. There was one bathroom on each floor, and you were given one opportunity to use it each day. If you had to go more than once, well, it was best to keep a bottle at your seat and try not to make a mess of things when you used it. There was a thirty-minute break for lunch in the middle of the shift.

Then there was one more thing about working for Mr. Blanck and Mr. Harris that it was best for the girls to try not to think about, and that was the business of the fires. The two men owned another garment factory, known as Diamond Waist. There had been two fires there, in 1907 and 1910; and there had been two at Triangle in 1902.

After every fire, the city inspectors would order the owners to install the modern sprinkler systems, but somehow they never got around to complying. They never got around to complying with any of the other safety measures the inspectors wanted them to make either.

The Asch Building was equipped with four elevators, for example, which would help the 720 Triangle workers evacuate in the event of a fire, but only two of them were working. There were two stairways too. One of them, on the Washington Street side of the building, was open. But the other, on the side facing Greene Street, was kept locked—the better to stop the girls and inspect their bags at the end of the day, to make sure they weren't stealing anything. The factory foreman had the only key. There was only one fire escape running the height of the building, but no one recalled how recently it had been inspected by city officials. If you looked out the southern-facing windows where the fire escape was, you couldn't help but notice all the rust that was covering it—one very good reason not to look out that window.

What there also were on all three floors of the Triangle Shirtwaist Factory were scraps of cloth—lots and lots of scraps of cloth from all of the fabric that was cut there every day. The scraps were stowed in bins beneath the tables. All around the factory, there were also shirtwaists hanging like curtains. Factory rules forbade smoking in such an environment, but those rules weren't strictly enforced, and plenty of the managers would sneak off for a cigarette in a corridor, exhaling the smoke through the lapels of their jackets in the hope of concealing what they were doing.

No one will ever know if any of this was on the minds of the estimated 600 Triangle workers who were required to work on Saturday, March 25, 1911, when they arrived for their comparatively short shift. They reported at 8:00 a.m. and would be free to leave at 4:45 p.m. By 4:40 p.m., many of the girls had already begun putting on their coats in anticipation of getting home in time for dinner with their families. They had just five minutes to go.

If the working conditions were miserable for the employees at the Triangle Shirtwaist Factory, they had the small consolation of knowing that at least they were not alone. The garment-making industry was a booming one in New York, and there were hundreds of factories employing tens of thousands of people. Shirtwaist makers like Blanck and Harris alone employed 30,000 people. Cloak makers employed another 60,000. Few of the factories were any better than the Triangle factory, and for that reason, the workers didn't even call them factories. They called them sweatshops.

Like the Triangle sweatshop, the garment industry as a whole was overwhelmingly female, with women and girls making up 70 percent of the employees—which suited the owners fine, since every additional female employee was one more rock-bottom three- to four-dollar daily salary they could pay. The arrangement suited the female employees much less well, and after a while, they decided to do something about it. In 1900, some of them formed a workers' group called the International Ladies' Garment Workers' Union (ILGWU). In 1903, another group, the Women's Trade Union League (WTUL), followed.

The purpose of the groups, known as labor unions, was simple: A factory owner could easily refuse to give one woman or one girl a raise; he could dock her pay for showing up late; he could tell her that she could not leave her machine to go to the bathroom when she needed to go. But he couldn't tell them all at once. If the workers got together, they could demand better pay, better working conditions, shorter days, and if the owners objected, well, the women would simply walk out and go on strike. Let the owners try to make their money then, without a single worker setting foot inside their miserable factories.

The mere threat of a strike, of course, turned out not to be enough to move the owners, so in November 1909, the unions decided to show their muscle. They called a great meeting at the Cooper Union Hall in downtown New York, the same place that a former United States congressman named Abraham Lincoln had delivered an address against slavery in 1860, launching him toward the presidency. The unions invited Samuel Gompers, head of the American Federation of Labor (AFL)—which organized unions in multiple industries across the entire country—as the featured speaker. Also in attendance, but merely in the audience, was Clara Lemlich, a petite, twenty-three-year-old immigrant who had been born in Ukraine in 1886, moved to the United States with her family when she was a girl and, like so many other new arrivals, found work in the garment industry.

Almost from the start, Lemlich was seen as a troublemaker by the owners. She spoke out about the ILGWU, recruited new members and spread the word about the rights of the workers. In 1907, she helped organize a successful strike at one small sweatshop—but she paid a price. The owners of the factory hired men to attack the workers as they marched, and Lemlich in particular was badly beaten. Still, as soon as she recovered, she went back to work and kept on organizing. She made it a point to be at Cooper Union for the most important workers' meeting of her lifetime.

The star speaker was, of course, Gompers, and he chose his words carefully. If he had told the workers they should strike, they surely would have. But he was smart enough to know that a strike took courage—that it could mean months without pay—and workers would not stick with it if it weren't their idea and their decision. He took the speaker's rostrum to thunderous applause and thus made clear from the start that he was there to guide, not to instruct.

"Mr. Shirtwaist Maker may be inconvenienced and his profits may be diminished if you girls and boys go out on strike," he said. "And mind you, I don't know whether a strike is necessary, but there is something greater than the convenience or the profits of Mr. Shirtwaist Maker at stake. There are the lives and the futures of the men and women in this work!"

He went on that way for a while, and the crowd roared and cheered at what he had to say. When he was done, the next speaker prepared to take the rostrum, but he never got to say so much as a word. In the middle of the crowd, Clara Lemlich popped up and announced, "I just wanted to say a few words!"

Some people recognized her voice; many others didn't. But they all recognized that what they were hearing was something different because the voice belonged not to a man like Gompers, who worked in an office, even if he worked on their behalf. It was the voice of a young woman—a young woman from the factory floor who knew what a fourteen-hour-day for three dollars pay with but a single bathroom break felt like.

"Get up on the platform!" someone called out. Other voices shouted in agreement. Rather than wait while Lemlich wove her way through the crowded hall—doing the sideways shimmy of the sweatshop—the people around her lifted her over their heads and then handed her off to the ones in front of them, who passed her on farther until the featherweight young woman was fairly deposited straight on the rostrum. She wasted little time—and spoke few words—making clear what she believed needed to be done.

"I have listened to all the other speakers and I have no further patience for talk!" she announced as the crowd cheered. "I am a working girl, one of those striking against intolerable conditions. I am tired of listening to speakers who talk in generalities." The cheer rose again, this time louder. "What we are here for is to decide whether or not to strike. I make a motion that we go out in a general strike!" At that, the cheers fairly rattled the hall, with cries of "Yes!" and "Strike!"

That strike, called the Uprising of the 20,000, began fast and hit hard. All over the city, sweatshops emptied. The owners tried to hire substitute workers, but the strikers marched in picket lines in front of their buildings, preventing anyone from crossing. It was a stalemate in which no one made money—not the strikers, not the owners—but the strikers were determined. Soon the newspapers began to take notice, visiting the workers on the line and reporting on the stand they were taking. After that, the lawmakers in city hall and in the state capitol in Albany began hearing things too and wondering if it might at last be time to pass some laws to regulate the industry and prevent this kind of unpleasantness in the future.

That threat, plus the lost money, at last broke the owners' will. The smaller sweatshops gave in first—promising the workers a bit more pay, slightly shorter days, even allowing them to form their own labor unions inside the factory. The bigger ones followed. The miserably awful sweatshops would remain miserably awful—if a bit less so as a result of the stand the workers took.

There was only one holdout—the Triangle Shirtwaist Factory. Blanck and Harris were not about to be told how to run their business. They hired women they knew to pose as passersby and pick fights with the picketers. They hired prizefighters—men who made their living fighting other men in front of spectators—to beat up the picketers. They paid policemen bribes to walk by at just that moment and arrest not the men but the women for causing a public disturbance.

At last, in February, Blanck and Harris gave in. A little. After three months with no pay, the battered women and girls of the Triangle sweatshop agreed to go back to work, in return for the same promises of slightly better pay and slightly better working conditions the other factories had offered their workers. There would be no changes made to the stairways or the elevators in the Asch Building—and the bins of fabric scraps would remain just as full as ever.

Which brings us back to that March Saturday in 1911. Many of the women on the eighth floor of the Triangle Shirtwaist Factory had already collected their purses and put on their coats and wraps in anticipation of the thirty-eight-degree chill outside when, at precisely 4:40 p.m., the flash of light in the southeast corner of the room caught their attention. Nobody would ever know which rag bin had birthed the flame that produced the flash—a flame that would soon grow much, much bigger. Nobody would ever know what the spark had been either—a discarded match or a tip of glowing ash from a forbidden cigarette, most likely.

Whatever the cause, the fire in the southeast bin grew fast, almost instantly spreading to other bins, and then igniting the shirtwaists hanging everywhere. The cry of "Fire!" went out across the room, and the workers who hadn't seen the flash when it happened saw the flames now. All of them leapt toward the exits—struggling to make their way down the narrow aisles. A floor manager whose job it was to grab the eighth-floor fire hose at the first whiff of smoke did just that, hoisting the heavy hose off the wall and twisting its metal valve. But the valve was rusted shut and the hose was rotted through, and he tossed it on the floor and sprang for the exits too.

A bookkeeper in a small office just off the main room picked up a telephone to alert the rest of the factory—or as much as could be alerted. There was a phone connection only to the tenth floor, where, as it happened, Blanck and Harris themselves were present, having brought their children and a governess with them—a visit to the fathers' place of business being an instructive outing for a Saturday afternoon. No telephone alert could go to the ninth floor, but that hardly mattered, because no sooner had the flames begun to spread on the eighth than they burst out the windows and flashed upward. The sight of them was impossible to miss from just one floor above.

On all three floors, there was a frenzy of activity. The tenth floor was equipped with a stairway to the roof and the workers, the owners, the children and the governess swarmed toward it. The eighth and ninth floors had just the one open stairway and the two working elevators. The foreman who had the key to the second stairway was one of the first people to make it down the other one and out to safety—taking the key with him.

Some of the terrified workers tried to open the locked door anyway, found it impossible and were crushed against it by the others behind them. The workers lucky enough to make it to the open stairway flung the door open and poured inside, but the stairs were not nearly wide enough to accommodate so many people at once—especially people who were wearing their bulky winter coats—and the stairway was already filling with smoke. There were two operators manning the two elevators—Joseph Zito and Gaspar Mortillalo—and they quickly learned what was going on above, likely from the smell of smoke filling the shaft. They raced as fast as their elevator cars could carry them to the burning floor, where the workers jammed inside as soon as the doors opened. When the car could hold no more, they descended, promising to return.

They did return, a few more times. But after that they could do no more. Fire can warp metal if it gets hot enough, and the rails on which the elevator cars ran soon bent. Both cars became trapped at the bottom of the shaft.

For both the eighth- and ninth-floor workers, there was still the fire escape, and they fought the flames toward the south-facing windows and clambered out. No more than twenty girls had climbed onto the rusted metal structure before it began buckling under their weight and pulling away from the building wall.

By now, it was clear to the people in the streets as well as to the students in the buildings at nearby New York University that something terrible was happening in the Asch Building. Fire alarms were pulled at multiple locations and fire trucks raced to the scene. The firefighters jumped down and began raising their ladders, which climbed steadily from ground level, up past the lower floors and finally to the sixth—but they stopped there. They had not been designed for a ten-story skyscraper and they could reach no higher. Police arrived at the same time as the firefighters and cordoned off the streets, which would prevent onlookers from getting too close to the building.

That was a very good thing, because just five minutes after the flames began, the first of the trapped people began appearing at the windows and flinging them open. Smoke and flames roared out behind them, and the people on the streets stared up in horror. It was clear to both the onlookers and the victims what was unfolding: the Triangle workers faced a mortal choice, an impossible choice, a choice that, in some ways, was no choice at all. They were going to die this afternoon—this very hour, probably this very minute. They knew that with a terrible certainty. They had no control over the fact of their death—only the manner of it. They could be consumed by the flames that had driven them to the windows, enduring surely an unimaginable pain in the final moments of their lives. Or they could jump. And so many decided to jump.

A man went first—one of the few men in the factory—and as the crowd saw what was happening they began shouting, "Don't jump!" Among the people on the street was Frances Perkins, a young woman who was then working for the Consumers League of New York, helping to ensure fair treatment for both the people who bought goods and the people who made them. Perkins had been having tea in the nearby home of a wealthy friend when a butler ran in and informed them that there was a fire in the Asch Building. She dashed out, ran to the corner of Washington and Greene Streets and, like the others, saw the people on the ledge. "Help is coming!" she screamed. But it was too late.

The man on the ledge leapt, fell and then struck the sidewalk with an awful force and noise, dying instantly. A man and a woman soon followed; they paused at the window, kissed once and then leapt together. Another girl with her hair and clothes already on fire jumped as well, but her dress caught on something and she dangled helplessly until the fabric burned through, and then she followed the others to the ground.

On the south wall of the building, away from the sight of most of the crowd, the fire escape gave way, spilling twenty girls at once to the sidewalk below. On the Greene and Washington Street sides, still more girls now appeared in the windows, looked and leapt, some of them landing on a heavy plate-glass covering on the sidewalk that let light into a basement space below. The glass was more than thick enough to allow pedestrians to walk on it, but not thick enough to support a falling human being—even a human being who was still a girl and might not have grown to her full adult size. One girl crashed through the glass and others followed her, and they died in the basement instead of on the sidewalk. Some of the girls had gotten lucky—perhaps—having appeared at the few windows below which the firefighters were standing with safety nets. But safety nets were useless today. The girls were falling too fast from too great a height and there were too many of them coming at once. The nets tore through and those girls died too.

There now followed still more bodies—a near rain of bodies, including five girls who leapt as one and died as one. A reporter would later write about learning a new sound that day—the sound of a speeding body hitting a solid sidewalk. But even people who were experienced with such horrors had no experience with the likes of this.

"It's the worst thing I ever saw," said one older police officer to a reporter on the scene.

Inside the building, girls who did not reach the windows tried another means of escape—tearing open the elevator doors and either leaping down the shaft or trying to slide down the cables. Those not killed by the impact of landing on the top of the cars would suffocate in the smoke and heat.

And then, almost as quickly as the fire began, it ended, winking out after just half an hour. The building itself was designed to be fireproof—with little or no wood in its design. Once the flames had raged through the three floors, consuming all the available fuel—the tables, the fabric, the benches, the human beings who until thirty minutes earlier had earned their living here—there was nothing left to keep them burning.

In the end, 146 people would lose their lives at the Triangle Shirtwaist Factory—123 girls and 23 men. Of those, 54 perished on the sidewalks; others in the elevator shafts; two survived that day but soon died of their injuries. Forty-nine of the workers "died in place," according to the official reports, meaning they burned to death within inches of the spot where they sat and worked every day of the week but Sunday. Nearly everyone who had been on the tenth floor would survive, many of them helped across the rooftops to the safety of other buildings by students from the university. Blanck and Harris and their children and their governess would be among the survivors.

In the days that followed the fire, fury swept New York in much the way the flames had swept the factory. It would take eleven days to identify most of the bodies, many of which were burned beyond recognition. Others were never identified at all and would eventually be buried together under a memorial stone in the Cemetery of the Evergreens in Brooklyn. On April 5, the day of the funerals for the unidentified victims, a cold day made worse by a persistent rain, 120,000 demonstrators set off on a march through New York City, beginning in Washington Square, adjacent to the Asch Building. The last of them had to wait four hours in the rain just for the chance to begin the march. Up to 280,000 other New Yorkers lined the somber parade route.

The state government did what governments often do only after a terrible tragedy has claimed lives, which was to begin to take the corrective steps they should have taken long before. The governor appointed a fire investigation committee that, in its first year, heard from 222 witnesses and investigated 1,836 factories in twenty industries statewide. Fifteen new laws were passed in just that first year and more than sixty overall would be passed before the end of 1913. The measures called for a maximum of a fifty-four-hour workweek, shorter workdays, limits on child labor, more breaks, better bathrooms and lunch rooms, and safer factories with sprinklers, handheld fire extinguishers, and more and wider stairways and fire escapes. New York's laws would soon become models for national laws.

In 1913, the federal government established the U.S. Department of Labor to ensure workers' safety and rights. In 1933, President Franklin Roosevelt would appoint Frances Perkins—who had rushed to the fire from her nearby tea—as the head of the department, making her the first woman to serve as a member of a president's cabinet. She would hold that position for twelve years—longer than any secretary of labor in history—and would go on to implement many of the reforms she had worked for even before the Triangle fire. Clara Lemlich was banned from the garment industry by the owners, making it impossible for her to visit factories and organize. So she would redirect her energies to helping working women get the vote—another important step in social justice.

Harris and Blanck were indicted for manslaughter, but in a criminal trial that lasted twenty-three days and heard from 150 witnesses, the prosecution failed to prove that the men actually knew that the door to the second stairway was locked. They were acquitted and walked free. Shortly after, they were found liable for the deaths and injuries in a second, civil trial—one that carried no risk of jail time—and ordered to pay a sum of $75 per life lost. Before the fire ever happened, however, they had bought an insurance policy that would protect them in such a situation, paying them $400 per life. They thus made a profit of $325 per killed worker—or close to $50,000 in total—when all the sums were paid. (That's the equivalent of $1.3 million at 2019 rates.) Blanck and Harris would go on to open other factories, one of them within days of the fire, and would once again be found to be locking doors to stairways, though now, at least, there were laws to punish them.

But if the men responsible for the fire would pay only a tiny fraction of the price the people who died that day paid, they would at least suffer the judgment of history—their despised names becoming symbols of the suffering too many laborers of their time faced. The women and men who stood up to them before the fire and the others who have continued standing up to people like them since—continuing to fight for safe conditions and decent wages—can never bring back the 146 victims who died, but they continue, in important ways, to give those deaths meaning.

Rosa Parks with the Reverend Martin Luther King Jr. in 1955.

FOUR

The Montgomery Bus Boycott
1955–1956

YOU KNOW A country has lost its way when it has laws that prevent people from playing together. In the United States in the early 1900s, there were a lot of laws that did just that. Most of the people the laws affected were children. They couldn't play together in public parks or in schools or on sports teams, and they absolutely, definitely could not play together in swimming pools. The authorities wouldn't even consider the matter of the swimming pools.

None of this meant that kids had to play completely alone; they could certainly play in groups—but only in certain kinds of groups. The white children could play with other white children and the Black children could play with other Black children, but there was to be absolutely no mixing. Even if people wanted to mix—and plenty of children did—it was difficult. The schools were segregated just like the parks and pools and sports teams, with only white children allowed to live in the neighborhoods with the better schools and Black children limited to the poorer areas with schools that were older and had fewer teachers and books and sports equipment. A school day spent with people only of your own color would be followed by evenings and weekends that would pass in much the same racially divided way.

Over time, there were even laws that prevented adults of the two races from playing together. In Montgomery, Alabama, a city law was passed that said it would forever be "unlawful for white and colored persons to play together, or, in company with each other . . . in any game of cards, dice, dominoes, checkers, pool, billiards, softball, basketball, baseball, football, golf, track, and at swimming pools, beaches, lakes or ponds or any other game or games or athletic contests, either indoors or outdoors."

That was another thing: back in the days when there were no-playing laws, people often used other terms to refer to Black people. They used "Negro" or "colored"—terms that are offensive today. And they used much, much worse words—ugly words meant to hurt and humiliate. It was mostly—but not entirely—in the southern part of the United States that there were formal laws keeping the races apart. And it was mostly—but not entirely—in the ninety years following the Civil War, from 1865 to 1955, that these laws were passed. Black people had won their freedom from slavery as a result of the war, so the laws, called Jim Crow laws—named after a Black character mockingly portrayed by white performers in traveling shows—were imposed by white politicians and policymakers to ensure that the races stayed separate.

The Jim Crow laws often had to keep up with developing technology. In the era before Southern cities had buses, for example, there were no rules to keep bus passengers separated by race, the way they were kept separate on trains. But once bus service was introduced, the rules were promptly written.

A lot of white people in Southern cities would have forbidden Black people from riding on buses at all, but that wasn't possible. Most white people had better-paying jobs than Black people, so they generally had more money and were likelier to own their own cars. Black people were much more dependent on buses. And the bus companies, in turn, were dependent on the ten-cent fares all of their passengers paid. If you refused the dimes that Black people were willing to spend, you'd soon go bankrupt. In Montgomery, Black people made up 75 percent of the bus ridership—but the local laws still made it hard on them.

First, while all passengers had to enter through the front door of the bus so that they could drop their money in the coin box next to the driver's seat, after Black people had paid they were required to get back off, walk around the bus and enter through the rear door. Once they were aboard, they then had to contend with the matter of getting a seat. There were thirty-six seats on most buses. The ten in the front were reserved for white riders; the ten in the back were the "colored section," set aside for Black riders. The sixteen seats in the middle were for both races—though Black and white people were not allowed to sit side by side or even in the same row.

If the bus was completely filled and white passengers entered, Black riders were required to give up their seats and stand in the back. In the event the bus got too full even for people to stand, Black passengers could be told to get off, no matter where the bus was or how far they'd have to walk to get to their destination, to make room for more white riders.

Those were the rules, and the drivers—all of whom were white—would enforce them. If anyone disobeyed, the driver would pull over and summon a police officer.

Some of the drivers were stricter about the segregation rules than others, and some were downright spiteful. James Blake was one of the spiteful ones. One day in 1943, a thirty-year-old Black seamstress named Rosa Parks boarded Blake's bus. She paid her bus fare, dropping her ten cents in the coin box, then got off to walk around to the back door so she could board and take her seat—if there was one in the colored section. But she never got the chance. Blake closed the front door and simply drove off without her.

There was nothing Parks could do—there was rarely anything Black people could do when they had been mistreated by white people in the Jim Crow South except tolerate it and hope things would get better in the future. But Parks did make herself a promise: that she would never again ride on a bus driven by James Blake. She made good on that promise too—until twelve years later, on Thursday, December 1, 1955.

Maybe she just didn't notice who was behind the wheel when she got aboard; maybe she was in a hurry and could not afford to wait for the next bus. Whatever it was, at 6:00 p.m. that day, after she had finished work at the Montgomery Fair department store, she once again found herself on Blake's bus. This time she got a seat—in the first row of the middle section. She wanted only to be able to go home and enjoy her evening. That, as it turned out, would not be what happened.

Rosa Parks—born Rosa McCauley in 1913—never expected anyone to make life easy for her. A Black girl in that era would not have the opportunities for education or employment that would be available to a white person, or even to a Black man. Parks thus kept her expectations in check while aiming as high as she possibly could, and her parents helped.

Her mother was a teacher in a Black school and her father was a carpenter, and they made sure their daughter attended the rural public schools near their home in Tuskegee, Alabama. When she was eleven, after her parents divorced, Parks and her mother moved to a community just outside of Montgomery, and she began attending a school known formally as the Montgomery Industrial School for Girls—and informally as Miss White's School for Girls, which simply sounded friendlier.

Parks hoped to be a teacher like her mother, and after she graduated from Miss White's, she enrolled at the Alabama State Teacher's College High School. But she never finished her education there. Her grandmother grew ill and then her mother did, and she had to stay away from school to care for them too often. Her ambition to be a teacher would thus not be fulfilled. Still, she was a fine seamstress, and knew she could always get work sewing and tailoring fine clothes for customers who had the money to buy them. It wasn't teaching, but there was something quietly appealing about the work.

In 1932, when she was only nineteen, Rosa McCauley married a barber named Raymond Parks, and she moved to Montgomery, where he lived. Like Rosa, Raymond had not finished high school, but he read extensively and was deeply interested in—and knowledgeable about—public affairs, especially the Black struggle for equal rights. He was also a member of the National Association for the Advancement of Colored People (NAACP), an organization founded in 1909 to fight for equality between the races, and he encouraged his new wife to join. Rosa did and was elected secretary. It was the only leadership position that was open to a woman, and while she might have liked an even loftier role, she took what she could get because it meant she could make more of a difference.

Over the years, Rosa and Raymond worked on many issues with the NAACP, including the trial of the Scottsboro Boys, nine Black boys from thirteen to nineteen years old, who were wrongly accused of attacking two white women on a train. They also worked to help register Black voters—a job that was not easy, because in the Jim Crow South there were laws directed at Black people that required them to pay special taxes or take special reading tests before they would be allowed to vote.

Parks herself had to return to the registrar's office three times before she was finally allowed to become a voter, but she persisted because she was determined to have a voice in choosing the elected officials who would make the laws that would govern her life.

Among the stubbornest of those laws was the one that continued to keep the buses segregated. In March 1955, a fifteen-year-old Black high school student named Claudette Colvin was arrested on a Montgomery bus for refusing to give up her seat to a white man. She worked in the youth division of the NAACP, and the organization defended her, filing a lawsuit appealing her arrest and conviction and arguing that they violated the United States Constitution, which guaranteed all Americans—Black or white—equal protection of the laws. The group had been looking for a case like Colvin's that could be publicized around the country as a symbol of the unjust segregation laws, and Colvin was happy to do the work necessary to be part of the campaign.

But the NAACP soon learned that she was pregnant without being married. That was a difficult matter for Colvin and her family. Still, it made her arrest no less unjust and the segregation laws no less wrong. The NAACP was worried, however. White people who were opposed to integrating the buses would likely dismiss Colvin as a careless girl—a bad girl—and they would tell themselves that they needn't give any thought to someone like her. The NAACP would defend her no matter what, and it filed the lawsuit challenging her arrest and conviction, but the group still needed to wait for someone who could help lead the charge to desegregate the buses.

Then, on December 1 of that same year, at the end of a long work-day, Rosa Parks climbed aboard James Blake's bus.

She chose the aisle seat in the fifth row—the first row behind the "whites only" section. A sign above her row read COLORED SECTION— indicating that Black people were allowed to sit there but only if no white passengers needed the seat. The seat next to Parks and the other two across the aisle were occupied by Black passengers.

For the first two stops, the trip was uneventful, but at the third stop, in front of the Empire Theater, several white passengers got on and there was no place for them to sit in the all-white section. Blake got up from his seat and moved the COLORED SECTION sign one row back, which meant that Parks and the other three people in the fifth row were suddenly where they didn't belong.

"Y'all better make it light on yourselves and let me have those seats," Blake said to them.

The other three Black passengers stood and moved out into the aisle. Parks did not; instead, she slid over to the window seat. Blake looked down at her.

"Are you going to get up?" he asked.

"No," Parks answered simply.

"Well," he said, "I'm going to have you arrested."

Parks looked at him squarely and spoke to him calmly. "You may do that," she said.

Blake hopped down from the bus, found a pay phone and called the police station, where an officer sent out a radio alert to all the police in the area. Leroy Pierce, a twenty-eight-year-old motorcycle patrolman, was the officer closest to the Empire Theater. He pulled up next to the bus and asked what the problem was.

"I'm having trouble with a Black female passenger sitting in the white section of the bus," Blake said.

Pierce and Blake climbed aboard the bus, where Parks was still waiting quietly in her seat. Two more officers in a patrol car then arrived and entered the bus as well; all four of them clustered near Parks. They asked her if she would move and she said no. One of the newly arrived officers then touched her on the shoulder and said, "You're now under arrest for violation of city ordinance for not sitting in the proper place." Parks still would not move, so the officer reached down and took hold of her as if he were helping her out of the seat. This time she cooperated; it was clear that if she did not, his helping her out of the seat would turn to forcibly yanking her out.

The three officers and Parks left the bus, and when they were outside, she turned to one of them and asked, "Why do you push us around so?"

The officer answered with surprising honesty. "I don't know," he confessed. "But the law's the law and you're under arrest."

Rosa Parks—seamstress, activist, forty-two-year-old department store worker who began the evening only wanting to get home for dinner with her husband and then decided it was time to take a stand—was taken to the police station. She was fingerprinted and then photographed, holding a sign with the number 7053 on it—the identification number for what was now her criminal record.

Prisoner number 7053 would not remain in police custody long. Word quickly spread about what had happened, and Edgar Nixon, the president of the local chapter of the NAACP, came to the police station and bailed her out. There was no mystery about how the case would end: Parks would be expected to appear in court the following Monday, December 5, where she would be fined ten dollars for breaking city laws and would be required to pay another four dollars in court costs. But what would happen beyond the courtroom was another matter.

The night of Parks's arrest, Nixon and other NAACP officials got together to discuss the matter, and also contacted the Reverend Ralph

Abernathy, a minister and civil rights leader in Montgomery. Abernathy was mentor to another, younger minister, the Reverend Martin Luther King Jr. Just twenty-six years old, King was a compelling speaker who had moved to Montgomery only the year before to become pastor of the Dexter Avenue Baptist Church. The two ministers and the NAACP leaders quickly decided what had to be done.

The buses were sources of humiliation and subjugation for Black people everywhere in Montgomery. If they could not change that fact, if the white leaders of the city would not treat Black passengers and white passengers equally, then there would *be* no more Black passengers. Let the city officials figure out how to keep their buses running if Black people quit paying to ride them. Instead of relying on buses, the Black residents of Montgomery would walk, they would bicycle, they would organize car pools. The ones who could afford the luxury of a taxi—which cost forty cents per ride, or four times as much as a bus fare—would get around that way too. The buses, however, would be off-limits.

The boycott needed a leader and the group decided that the job would go to King. Since he was new to town, the white leaders had not gotten to know him yet, which meant they did not know his temperament and could not anticipate his moods or plans. Just as important, they had not had a chance to try to intimidate him yet.

Nixon stayed awake that first night running off 35,000 copies of a leaflet that would be distributed all over Montgomery. The language was clear and simple and strong:

> *Another Negro woman has been arrested and thrown in jail because she refused to get up out of her seat on the bus for a white person to sit down. It is the second time since the Claudette Colvin case that a Negro woman has been arrested for the same thing. This has to be stopped.*

Negroes have rights, too, for if Negroes did not ride the buses, they could not operate. Three-fourths of the riders are Negroes, yet we are arrested, or have to stand over empty seats. If we do not do something to stop these arrests, they will continue. The next time it may be you, or your daughter, or mother.

This woman's case will come up on Monday. We are, therefore, asking every Negro to stay off the buses Monday in protest of the arrest and trial. Don't ride the buses to work, to town, to school, or anywhere on Monday. You can afford to stay out of school for one day if you have no other way to go except by bus. You can also afford to stay out of town for one day. If you work, take a cab, or walk. But please, children and grown-ups, don't ride the bus at all on Monday. Please stay off of all buses Monday.

All weekend long, the organizers worked, and when Monday arrived, every part of the boycott went exactly as they hoped it would. More than 90 percent of Black riders went nowhere near the buses, and Black taxi drivers cooperated by lowering their fares to just ten cents for any of the boycotters. It was a huge success, beyond what the organizers had dared to expect. That night, they met at the Holt Street Baptist Church to decide what their next steps should be. The *Montgomery Advertiser* newspaper had learned about the meeting and ran an ominous-sounding story about it: "A 'top secret' meeting of Montgomery Negroes . . . is scheduled at 7 p.m. Monday at Holt Street Baptist church for 'further instructions' in an 'economic reprisal' campaign."

But there was no reprisal involved. There was no retribution or spite in what the Black people in Montgomery were doing. They were seeking what was right and fair, nothing more. And there was nothing top secret about the sentiments that would be voiced in the church— most powerfully by King.

"We're going to work with grim and bold determination to gain justice on the buses in this city," he declared. "And we are not wrong, we are not wrong in what we are doing. If we are wrong, the Supreme Court of this nation is wrong. If we are wrong, the Constitution of the United States is wrong . . . We are going to work together! We are going to stick together! Right here in Montgomery."

Before King was even finished speaking, it was clear to many in the church what would happen next: The boycott would not be a one-day affair. It would go on—and on and on and on, as long as it took for the city to crack and for justice to prevail.

Montgomery's Black citizens heard that call and embraced the boycott, and it did go on. They continued to walk and carpool and ride their bikes—peaceably, doggedly. Reprisals and retaliation did come, but they came from the white community. Parks, who continued to work with Nixon, Abernathy, King and the rest of the organizers, was fired from her job, as were many other boycotters. Firebombs were thrown at King's and Abernathy's houses and at several Black churches. Snipers fired guns at buses—an expression of white anger even though there weren't any Black people aboard. Local officials pressed insurance companies to cancel the policies on any cars used in the car pools, so the British firm Lloyd's of London stepped in and insured each car so the owners would be paid back if anything happened to it.

The boycott continued through the winter and the spring and the summer of 1956. Parks had appealed her criminal conviction, and her case crept up through the court system, headed—one day—for the Supreme Court of the United States, the highest court in the land, where the justices might rule that the Montgomery law and all similar bus segregation laws everywhere in the country were unconstitutional. For now, though, it was moving very slowly and any resolution would take years. But there was another case too, known as

Browder v. Gayle, that was speeding along by comparison. Browder was Aurelia S. Browder, a Black woman living in Montgomery who was also challenging the segregated bus law; she was joined by three other plaintiffs, including Claudette Colvin, all Black Montgomery women forced to ride the city's segregated buses. Gayle was William A. Gayle, the mayor of Montgomery.

In June 1956, a federal court in Alabama, familiar with the stand the Black people in Montgomery were making and the momentum they were gathering, ruled in favor of the plaintiffs, deciding that the segregated bus laws violated the Constitution. That was good news—but short-lived, because Gayle and the city promptly appealed to a higher court, which meant the segregation law would stay in place and the boycott would continue until the Supreme Court finally, decisively ruled.

On November 13, 1956, the court did rule. The justices upheld the decision of the lower court. Segregation on buses in Montgomery or anywhere else in the United States was a violation of the Constitution; it was a legal wrong, a moral wrong, and it would be neither tolerated nor permitted ever again. That night, King spoke to a grateful and relieved congregation at the Holt Street Baptist Church.

"These eleven months have not been easy," he said. "Our feet have often been tired and our automobiles worn. But we have kept going in the faith that in our struggle, we have cosmic companionship and that, at bottom, the universe is on the side of justice."

The universe was, as was the Constitution, but the boycotters' feet and cars would suffer for another five weeks, until, on December 20, the official order arrived in Montgomery from the court, overturning the local laws. The boycott at last ended—in its 381st day.

Segregation itself did not end in Montgomery that day, nor did it end in Alabama or anywhere else in the South. It endured too in many other parts of the United States. The struggle for full integration was destined to be a long—and still-incomplete—one. Martin Luther King Jr. would live less than twelve years after the boycott before he was killed by an assassin in 1968. Parks and her husband would be unable to find jobs in Montgomery, where white employers refused to hire them, so they moved first to Hampton, Virginia, where she found a job at a Black college. They then moved to Detroit, and Parks found work in the office of Congressman John Conyers—a position she held until 1988.

As history would unfold, the seemingly modest woman who could take no more injustice would become one of the most celebrated people in the long history of civil liberties. States and cities would declare holidays to honor her; Detroit's 12th Street was renamed Rosa Parks Boulevard. In 1996, President Bill Clinton awarded her the Presidential Medal of Freedom; in 1999, the United States Congress awarded her the Congressional Gold Medal. And after she died, on October 24, 2005, President George W. Bush ordered that flags around the country be lowered to half-mast, and both Detroit and Montgomery marked the front seats of all of their city buses with black ribbons—leaving them empty as a sign of respect until after Parks's funeral was complete.

Racial, religious and cultural tensions remain in the United States. Black people and white people—as well as Asian people and Hispanic people and Christian people and Jewish people and Muslim people and all other people—make an agreement by living in America. It is an agreement that color and faith and nationality do not matter here, that we are all equal. We still don't honor that agreement as well as we should. But it's one that sits as the very center of who we are.

The Reverend Martin Luther King Jr. leads a crowd during the March on Washington.

FIVE

The March on Washington
1963

THERE WAS NOTHING quite like the day in August 1963 that a white man accidentally stepped on Hazel Mangle Rivers's foot. It was surely not the first time that a white man—or any white person—had accidentally stepped on Hazel's foot, but this time was different for a lot of reasons.

For one thing, she was in Washington, D.C., when it happened. Hazel never been there before—had never even been as far north as Washington in her entire life, and it had been a long life so far. She wouldn't say exactly *how* long that life was when the reporter from the *New York Times* talked to her—and that was another thing special about that day in 1963: When else would a reporter from the *New York Times* talk to an ordinary person like Hazel? But if she ducked the question when the reporter asked, she did disclose that she'd been around long enough that she had eight children back home, and after taking a moment to assemble all of their names in her head, she rattled them off. By the next day, their names would appear in a *New York Times* story along with hers.

"Back home" for Hazel and her family was Birmingham, Alabama—a pretty enough city but not a terribly appealing one if you were Black, like she was. There were 340,000 people in Birmingham, about 40 percent of whom were Black. For all of the residents, but especially for that 40 percent, 1963 had been an absolutely miserable year.

The trouble had been simmering for a long time—all of it the result of Birmingham's laws that kept the races apart, denying Black people equal access to schools, jobs, homes, buses, hotel rooms, public bathrooms, public drinking fountains, lunch counters and even stores if the owners chose. The stores were a tricky matter because the owners needed the money Black customers were willing to spend as much as they needed the white customers' money. So they would compromise: Black people could shop in their stores, though they would have to wait for all the white customers to be served first. They were welcome to shop for clothes if that's what the store sold, but they would certainly not be allowed to try them on first. A white customer would never buy any article of clothing a Black customer had worn for even an instant.

There was only so much of this the Black population was willing to take, and lately they'd been pushing back—speaking out and even demonstrating for civil rights. Some of the white population supported them, agreeing that the local laws were wrong and just plain immoral. But too many others disagreed, and they responded violently. Demonstrators were harassed and attacked. Worse, Black homes, churches and schools were targeted by homemade bombs—so often in fact that the city was given the nickname Bombingham.

Finally, in 1963, the Black residents decided they had had enough. On April 3 of that year, the Alabama Christian Movement for Human Rights (ACMHR) joined hands with the Southern Christian Leadership Conference (SCLC)—the group led by the young Reverend Martin Luther King Jr. that was formed during the Montgomery bus boycott of 1955. The two organizations rallied Birmingham's Black community to stage a series of peaceful demonstrations throughout the city—holding marches and public meetings, conducting sit-ins at libraries and lunch counters until they were allowed to check out a book or order a meal like anyone else. Taking their lesson from Montgomery, they would also boycott all the local stores: if the owners didn't treat the Black shoppers like anyone else, they could do without the Black shoppers' money.

The city hit back hard. The local government could not force Black residents to shop where they didn't want to, but they could try to prevent them from conducting demonstrations. They asked the state government to issue an injunction forbidding the demonstrations—declaring them illegal—and on April 10 that ruling was granted. The injunction itself was illegal—a violation of the First Amendment of the United States Constitution that guarantees all Americans the free-dom of speech, religion, the press and the right "peaceably to assemble and petition the government for a redress of grievances." That was the founding fathers' way of saying, "You want to demonstrate? Go demonstrate—just don't hurt anybody or break anything."

The Birmingham protesters weren't hurting a soul or breaking a thing. But the city officials were a different matter—especially the public safety commissioner, whose name was Eugene Connor, but who was better known as Bull Connor. When the demonstrations went on even after the injunction was issued, he ordered that King be arrested and locked up in Birmingham jail, where he was kept in solitary con-finement for eight days—held alone in a cell with no contact with any human being except a guard who brought him his meals. Worse, Connor dispatched his officers into the streets armed with clubs, fire hoses and trained police dogs—and told them to do their worst. The officers obeyed.

Water erupts from a fire hose at a speed exceeding seventy miles per hour. It can knock people to the ground or slam them up against walls and buildings hard enough to break bones. The German shepherds that were used as Birmingham's police dogs were able to bite with a force of 1,500 pounds of pressure per square inch, more than enough to grab and tear human flesh. And nobody needed any explanation about the damage a wooden club swung by an angry police officer could do.

Newspapers and televisions across America were filled with the scenes of the violence in Birmingham, as hundreds and then more than a thousand drenched, bleeding, broken protesters were thrown in police wagons, carried off to jail, locked up and labeled criminals for trying to exercise the simple freedom that the First Amendment promised them.

Finally, on May 10, with the nation outraged at the violence and the businesses in Birmingham going bankrupt for lack of Black customers, the leaders of the city had had enough. The federal government sent a representative to help negotiate a settlement and one was quickly reached: Birmingham's stores, restrooms, lunch counters, water fountains and more would all be desegregated within ninety days; in return the SCLC and ACMHR would call off their protests. Two more bombs went off the very next day: one at the hotel where King and the other SCLC leaders had stayed and another at the home of King's brother. That, however, would not stop the agreement from going into effect, and Birmingham would slowly return to an uneasy peace.

Something else, however, happened as a result of those five weeks of ugliness in one of the deepest parts of the old Deep South: the country had gotten a clear, honest, ugly look at itself—at an animal violence exhibited by white Americans that was far worse than the animal violence unleashed by the dogs. And the country didn't like what it saw.

Now, just three months later, on August 28, 1963, people were gathering again, for another demonstration—a far grander one. This time it wouldn't be just a few thousand residents of Birmingham gathering in the town center. This time it would be up to 250,000 Americans from all over the country pouring into Washington, D.C. Once again, most of them would be Black; once again, they would be campaigning for equal rights. Once again, they would face the danger of a violent backlash from an angry white majority.

But something felt different today too—strangely hopeful, strangely better, as if a powerful shifting were taking place.

That was the thing that Hazel Mangle Rivers noticed after she arrived in Washington, as part of the tens and tens of thousands who would be gathering here. She had traveled all night by bus, paying eight dollars for a ticket, or 10 percent of the eighty dollars her husband earned every week working as a truck driver. But it was worth it—especially in that moment, when she was making her way through the crowd and the white man accidentally stepped on her foot.

Hazel turned to look at the man; the man turned to look at her. And then he did something remarkable: he said, "Excuse me." Hazel's eyes widened and then she smiled.

"I said, 'Certainly,'" she told the *New York Times* reporter. "That's the first time that has ever happened to me. I believe that was the first time a white person has ever really been nice to me."

Yes, it seemed, something was definitely shifting.

It was always clear that if Black people wanted true equality, they would have to go to Washington to get it. Local demonstrations were having a powerful effect, but they were just that: local. If stores integrated in Birmingham, that did not mean they would in Biloxi. A bus boycott in Montgomery might not impress anyone in Mississippi. A true national remedy for racial injustice could only come if Washington stepped in and wrote new laws that the nation as a whole was bound to obey.

In 1963, just such a law was a tangible possibility. John F. Kennedy had been sworn in as president two years before and, as part of his campaign, had promised that a sweeping civil rights act would be passed by Congress. He made good on part of that promise, working with senators and representatives to see that a bill was written and introduced, but that's as far as a president could go. It was up to the senators and representatives themselves to pass the bill and only then could Kennedy sign it into law. At the moment, the bill was stalled in Congress, opposed by Southern senators and representatives, most from Kennedy's own Democratic Party.

What was needed was a push, and the idea of a march on the city of Washington was being talked about more and more. The horror in Birmingham had made things seem only more urgent, even to people who hadn't cared much about civil rights before. And there was one more thing that made 1963 just the right time for just the right action: it was the one-hundredth anniversary of the Emancipation Proclamation—the order that President Abraham Lincoln had signed in the thick of the Civil War, declaring slavery illegal in all of the rebellious states. (It was already illegal in the North.) Lincoln would surely be disappointed if he could come back and see the state of race relations in the nation a century later, so perhaps it was time to fix things in a way that would make the great emancipator proud.

The effort to stage a march was being led by A. Philip Randolph, head of the Negro American Labor Council. Twenty-two years earlier, in 1941, Randolph had threatened then-president Franklin Roosevelt with a similar gathering of perhaps 100,000 Black people if the president did not make sure that they were given an equal opportunity for jobs in the industries that were manufacturing military equipment for a second world war, which everyone suspected was coming to American shores soon.

Randolph shrewdly reached out initially to Eleanor Roosevelt, the president's wife, who was a vocal advocate of civil rights. Much of the time, what Eleanor insisted upon, Franklin did, and this time was no exception. Just days before the march was set to begin, he signed an executive order, decreeing that "there shall be no discrimination in the employment of workers in the defense industry or government because of race, creed, color or national origin . . ."

If the mere threat of a march was enough to move a president in 1941, Randolph reasoned that an actual march might move an entire Congress in 1963. In May, he officially announced that an "Emancipation March on Washington for Jobs" would take place sometime in October. King and the Southern Christian Leadership Conference were at the same time considering a similar demonstration they called the "March for Freedom." Instead of competing, the two groups decided to join hands and stage a combined "March on Washington for Jobs and Freedom." They agreed on one other thing too: that the event could not wait until October. It would have to happen in the summer, when the memory of Birmingham still burned and Congress would feel the pressure to act. Wednesday, August 28, before the Labor Day holiday, was chosen as the date.

King's and Randolph's groups quickly attracted the leaders of four other groups, including John Lewis, the fiery twenty-three-year-old head of the Student Nonviolent Coordinating Committee, and Roy Wilkins of the National Association for the Advancement of Colored People (NAACP). Those six groups attracted four more, including the National Catholic Conference for Interracial Justice and the American Jewish Congress.

Those later additions meant that now there were white faces and non-Christians involved in the mobilization. Civil rights are human rights, the involvement of the new members made clear. Freedom for

Black people would lift white people too; the ideals of the Christian organizers were embraced by Jews and Muslims and people of other faiths as well. In that spirit, the organizers quickly dispensed with the question of whether the march on Washington would be open only to Black people: it would not. White people would be allowed to march; indeed, they would be encouraged to march. The event would be open to "all Americans of good will." If you didn't fit into that category, well, maybe it was time to rethink who you were.

The planners of the March for Jobs and Freedom worked feverishly throughout the three months between May and August, establishing their headquarters in New York City, at 130th Street and Lenox Avenue, in the Black neighborhood of Harlem. Racing the calendar to August 28, they reached out to local chapters of the SCLC, the NAACP and other groups, urging them to rally people in their communities, churches, schools and places of business and tell them about the march. A twelve-page organizer's handbook was published and mailed out by the tens of thousands, announcing the march, explaining where and when it would be, what its goals were, how volunteers could get to Washington and where to stay when they were there.

The group encountered obstacles in those three months—some terrifying. Bomb threats were phoned in by anonymous callers— opponents of integration who had learned of the march and were determined to stop it. The threats were largely ignored. King was threatened with violence too—but he was used to that by now and shrugged it off.

Problems came from Washington as well. On June 22, President Kennedy invited King, Randolph and the other leaders to the White House to discuss his worries about the march—specifically that it might have precisely the opposite effect in Congress than intended, stirring up even more resistance among Southern segregationists. Kennedy was especially concerned that the marchers, who had still not decided on exactly where in the city of Washington the event would take place, were considering the grounds around the Capitol building itself, where the Congress met. That, Kennedy warned, could make the senators and representatives feel under siege, as if they were being surrounded and threatened with attack.

It was a legitimate worry, and the marchers quickly agreed to move the event to the space known as the National Mall, the massive span of grassy land between the Lincoln Memorial and the Washington Monument. The mall was informally known as "America's Front Yard," and if a place with a name like that wasn't the right spot for the national family to gather and campaign for the rights of all Americans, it was hard to see what would be.

But then the president went too far. He wanted the entire march postponed until some future date since he feared alienating Congress no matter what. "We want success in the Congress, not just a big show," he told them. No matter where exactly the march was held, it was simply "ill-timed."

King would have none of that.

"Frankly," the reverend told the president, "I have never engaged in any direct-action movement that did not seem ill-timed." The president had no answer; the march would continue on schedule.

There was a half-moon in Washington, D.C., on August 27, the night before the march was to begin, and the weather was uncharacteristically pleasant. Washington can be swampy in August—blisteringly hot and suffocatingly humid—but it was just sixty-three degrees before the sun rose, with a high temperature for the day forecast in the low eighties, and an equally low humidity that made the breeze refreshing instead of oppressive. Nature, it seemed, was smiling on the march.

For the organizers, that final night was a frenzy of planning, made much more frantic by a last-minute scare, when the sound system that would be needed for the speeches the next day mysteriously failed. The system had cost $19,000—more than $155,000 in 2019 money—and had been donated by the United Auto Workers union, which supported the march. It was the very best audio equipment available, the kind that would be needed to reach so huge a sea of marchers—and the kind that was not likely simply to fail by accident. It hadn't. The technicians quickly determined that the system had instead been sabotaged by people opposed to the march—and sabotaged so badly that they couldn't figure out how to fix it.

Walter Fauntroy, the head of the Washington chapter of the SCLC, placed an urgent phone call to the office of the United States attorney general, Robert Kennedy, President Kennedy's brother, pleading for government assistance.

"We have a couple hundred thousand people coming," he said. "Do you want a fight here after all we've done?"

Kennedy and his staff very much did not. They quickly dispatched technicians from the U.S. Army Signal Corps—electronics specialists who knew how to rig a reliable communications system on a muddy battlefield with bullets flying overhead and shells raining down. Within hours, they had solved the problem the march technicians couldn't, and had the sound system repaired.

Even before that work was done, the marchers were streaming into Washington. They'd been coming all day on the twenty-seventh and continued into the night. They arrived by bus, train, plane and car. More than 2,000 buses—450 from New York alone—made their way to Washington. At least half a dozen of them came from Birmingham, one of them bringing Hazel Mangle Rivers, mother of eight, who had never seen Washington before. There were at least twenty-one chartered trains and ten chartered planes and nobody knew how many cars, and they all kept arriving and disgorging their passengers by the tens and tens and tens of thousands.

The twenty-eighth may have been a Wednesday, but with the police warning of the arriving masses and with many businesses either closed or on short schedules to allow workers to attend the march and avoid the traffic, the sun rose on a city that actually had the feel of a Sunday. The day's events were scheduled to begin at 10:00 a.m. with the marchers massing at the Washington Monument and beginning their procession down Constitution Avenue and Independence Avenue, in two parallel streams, converging on the Lincoln Memorial by noon. TV cameras and newspaper reporters were everywhere, interviewing the marchers and telling their story to the nation. Spotters in helicopters hovered high above and radioed down the estimated crowd size: it was somewhere between 200,000 and 300,000. From on the ground it appeared that at least 60,000 of those people were white. Americans "of good will" were showing up.

The river of Black and white humanity flowed along, moving west until it reached the steps of the Lincoln Memorial. People gathered there, stretching back across the great landscaped parkland in front of the memorial, farther back along either side of the capital's vast reflecting pool, which measured more than three football fields long, and back farther toward the Washington Monument from which they'd come.

Performers appeared at the microphone on the steps of the Lincoln Memorial first. Gospel singer Mahalia Jackson sang; so did folk singers Peter, Paul and Mary, as did a young Bob Dylan—who would go on to become one of the giants of folk and rock music, but then was just a twenty-two-year-old newcomer with promising talent who was doing what he could to help an important cause. Opera singer Marian Anderson had been forbidden to perform in Washington's Constitution Hall in 1939 because of her race, so Eleanor Roosevelt had arranged for her to perform at the Lincoln Memorial; today she would perform there again, concluding the gathering after all of the speeches were done.

The Black comedian and commentator Dick Gregory spoke too, and mused at how far Black Americans had come in just the past three months. "The last time I saw this many of us," he said, "Bull Connor was doing all the talking."

But it was the speakers, the leaders, the visionaries of the march who the quarter million had come to see and hear. And they delivered.

Randolph was one of the first to speak and made it clear that if a quarter million could assemble today, more would be mobilized until justice was done. "We are gathered here for the largest demonstration in the history of this nation," he said. "Let the nation and the world know the meaning of our numbers. We are the advance guard of a massive moral revolution."

Lewis spoke too and—young student leader that he was—delivered the most blistering address of the day. "Where is the political party that will make it unnecessary to march in the streets of Birmingham?" he demanded. "Where is the political party that will protect the citizens of Albany, Georgia? To those who have said, 'Be patient and wait,' we have long said that we cannot be patient. We do not want our freedom gradually, but we want to be free now!"

But it was King—the speaker for whom speech was music and words were lyrics—who would make the greatest history on that warm and gentle day. It was King most of the people had come to hear, and at first it seemed they would not get much. His speech was supposed to last just four minutes and was written out on a sheet of paper in front of him. Some of his advisers had urged him to speak as the preacher he was; others had cautioned him to remain political, practical, to call for reforms in a way that would move Congress even if it moved the crowd less.

King began to read his speech aloud, and it was clear that he had chosen the safer route. The words were powerful, poetic even, but they were practical too. "In a sense, we've come to our nation's capital to cash a check," he said. "When the architects of our republic wrote the magnificent words of the Constitution and the Declaration of Independence, they were signing a promissory note to which every American was to fall heir. This note was a promise that all men—yes, Black men as well as white men—would be guaranteed the inalienable rights of life, liberty and the pursuit of happiness. . . . And so we've come to cash this check. . . . We have also come to this hallowed spot to remind America of the fierce urgency of now."

The crowd listened, and they paid attention as King followed his script. He echoed Lewis's idea that "this is no time to engage in the luxury of cooling off"; he reminded his listeners that white Americans should remember that "their freedom is inextricably bound to our freedom."

And then, from behind King, Mahalia Jackson called out. "Tell 'em about the dream, Martin," she said.

Most people didn't hear that, but King could not have missed it. Jackson knew of King's dream, and a few people there did too, people who were fortunate enough to have heard him speak about it before. But most of the 250,000 people in Washington had not.

Now King's posture changed. He held the sides of the lectern in the pose of a preacher; he paid no mind to the pages in front of him.

Clarence Jones, who worked with King on his speeches and was standing behind him as well, turned to the person standing next to him and said, "These people don't know it, but they're about ready to go to church."

And a church was indeed what the steps of the Lincoln Memorial became.

"I am not unmindful that some of you have come here out of great trials and tribulations," King said. "Some of you have come fresh from narrow jail cells. . . . You have been the veterans of creative suffering." The listeners knew that King had recently been confined to his own narrow jail cell, that he had suffered too. He went on:

"I say to you today, my friends, so even though we face the difficulties of today and tomorrow, I still have a dream. It is a dream deeply rooted in the American dream." The cadence of his voice increased, its volume modulated up.

"I have a dream that one day this nation will rise up and live out the true meaning of its creed: 'We hold these truths to be self-evident; that all men are created equal,'" he sang out as the crowd began to cheer.

"I have a dream," he said, "that one day on the red hills of Georgia, the sons of former slaves and the sons of former slave owners will be able to sit down together at the table of brotherhood." The crowd could see the red hills and feel the kinship at that table.

"I have a dream that one day even the state of Mississippi, a state sweltering with the heat of injustice, sweltering with the heat of oppression, will be transformed into an oasis of freedom and justice." The crowd could feel the heat of hate and glimpse the oasis that might replace it.

"I have a dream that my four little children will one day live in a nation where they will not be judged by the color of their skin but by the content of their character," King said, and the listeners could picture their own little children, their own grandchildren, who could share that dream.

"And if America is to be a great nation, this must be true," King called. "So let freedom ring, let freedom ring from the snow-capped Rockies of Colorado . . . from the curvaceous slopes of California. But not only that: Let freedom ring from the Stone Mountain of Georgia. Let freedom ring from . . . Lookout Mountain of Tennessee. Let freedom ring from every hill and molehill of Mississippi. From every mountainside, let freedom ring."

In Washington, King's own voice rang out, as did the cheers of the people behind him on the stage and the cheers from the quarter million before him, and he finished with one triumphant wish:

"When we allow freedom to ring, when we let it ring from every village and every hamlet, from every state and every city, we will be able to speed up that day when all of God's children, Black men and white men, Jews and gentiles, Protestants and Catholics, will be able to join hands and sing in the words of the old Negro spiritual, 'Free at last! Free at last! Thank God Almighty, we are free at last!'"

Then the preacher finished what had turned into a sixteen-minute sermon and stepped away from the dais—and nothing was ever the same again.

Dr. Martin Luther King Jr.'s words that day would become known simply as the "I Have a Dream" speech. It was seen on TV all around the planet, and the Voice of America radio station translated it into thirty-six languages and distributed it further, so that the world could learn that even when America lost its way in its long mission to be worthy of its founders' dreams, there were people who could point us back.

President Kennedy would never see the passage of the civil rights bill that the march on Washington was meant to advance. Less than three months later, he was killed by an assassin in Dallas, Texas.

Vice President Lyndon Johnson, who assumed the presidency that day, would succeed in getting the bill passed the next year—partly as a tribute to the lost Kennedy, and surely as a tribute to the power of King's words. The following year, Johnson would succeed again, securing passage of the Voting Rights Act, which meant that Black people could not legally be kept from the polls and would always have a voice in choosing the nation's leaders.

In the following years, Black people would move into schools and colleges and communities and jobs that had been closed to them before. The progress would be slow, uneven, with many setbacks, but it would continue all the same. Young John Lewis would go on to become Congressman John Lewis from Georgia, winning his first congressional election in 1986; he would be reelected sixteen times, most recently in 2018. Black senators, representatives, mayors and governors would be elected all over the country.

And one more important step would be taken too. On that day in 1963 when the march was held, few people gave any thought to a small Black boy, born in Hawaii, who was far too young to understand what was going on. He had been born only two years earlier and had been named after his father. When he was a little older though, the boy—Barack Hussein Obama—would learn about the march and would absorb its message, especially King's words about the importance of taking action, about the "fierce urgency of now." Forty-five years after the march, in 2009, he would make his own powerful history, being sworn in as President of the United States in the same city in which Dr. Martin Luther King Jr. had once spoken about his dream.

A protester faces off against a National Guardsman in front of the Hilton Hotel during the demonstrations.

SIX

The Democratic Convention
1968

NONE OF THE officers in the Chicago Police Department went into August 1968 expecting to arrest a pig. As things turned out, they did arrest a pig; it happened on August 23, a Friday, and as far as they knew, the pig didn't mind—though the pig didn't say either.

It was Jerry Rubin, the thirty-year-old activist and one of the founding members of the Youth International Party, or Yippies, who led the group that bought the pig and brought him to the city. They named him Pigasus, after the mythical winged horse Pegasus, and once they got him to Chicago, they took him to the grounds in front of the city's civic center and, in the presence of 250 demonstrators and spectators, nominated him for president.

"I, Pigasus," Rubin said, reading the pig's prepared text for him, "hereby announce my candidacy for the presidency of the United States."

That's more or less when the police intervened and arrested Rubin and six other demonstrators, charging them with disorderly conduct and violating a law against bringing livestock into the city. Pigasus was taken into custody too; he was not transported to jail with the humans, but instead to the Chicago Anti-Cruelty Society. One of the demonstrators explained to the police why they had chosen to nominate a pig for the highest office in the land:

"If we can't have him for president," he said, "we can have him for breakfast."

That was the way the Yippies did things: they were loud, they were silly, they were impossible to ignore—and they were deadly serious too. They were in Chicago for a much more important reason than simply staging a little public farce. It was the same reason that animated more than ten thousand other young people affiliated with different political groups—the Students for a Democratic Society (SDS), the National Mobilization Committee to End the War in Vietnam, the Black Panther Party, the People Against Racism, and more—when they also descended on Chicago in that broiling week, in that boiling year.

The demonstrators had come to Chicago because the Democratic Party was holding its national convention—which both parties held every four years to choose their presidential candidate—in the city's International Amphitheater. The convention would run for four days, from August 26 to 29, and its most important job would be to pick an actual candidate—a human candidate—to represent the party in that fall's presidential election. The month before, the Republican Party had held its own convention in Miami, Florida, and had nominated former vice president Richard Nixon as its candidate. The convention had gone smoothly: there were bands and balloons and happy demonstrations and the party emerged unified and convinced that it could win in the fall.

Things were very different—in some ways tragically different—on the Democratic side. Earlier in the year, most people had expected the president, Lyndon Johnson, who was a Democrat, to run for reelection. If he did, most of the other people in his party who wanted to be president would stand aside and wait their turn until 1972.

That was, in fact, how things started out, but they did not unfold as planned. Johnson had been a well-loved president only a few years before, partly because of the work he did to push for the passage of the Civil Rights Act of 1964 and the Voting Rights Act of 1965, ensuring equal rights for Black people. But since then, he had become exceedingly *un*popular—even despised, by many people. The reason was the war in Vietnam, which he had been waging since he assumed the presidency after the assassination of President Kennedy in 1963.

The Vietnam War was a bit like America's Civil War—a fight between the northern and southern halves of that Southeast Asian country. The South Vietnamese army was supported by the United States and the North—which wanted to impose a communist system on the country—by the Soviet Union, America's mortal enemy at the time. Unlike America's Civil War however, which most people in the United States agreed needed to be fought, many couldn't see what business America had meddling in Vietnam's business.

Part of the problem was that, from a military perspective, the war was not going well at all. It was expensive and it was bloody and America wasn't really winning it but wasn't really losing it either, so Johnson kept ordering that more and more young men be drafted into the army and sent to the other side of the world to fight. By 1968, more than 550,000 American soldiers were at war in the jungles of Vietnam, and so far, about 20,000 of them had been killed. Many more were expected to die before 1968 was over.

Early in the year, Eugene McCarthy, a Democratic senator from Minnesota, announced that despite Johnson's initial plans to run again, he would declare his candidacy too, promising to end the war. Thousands of young people campaigned for McCarthy—enough that in the first early test, the primary election in New Hampshire, he won 42 percent of the vote, not quite enough to beat Johnson's 48 percent but a far better showing than was expected. Johnson, deciding he might well lose his reelection bid, announced that, on second thought, he would not be running again and would instead retire at the end of his current term.

That threw the competition wide open, and Senator Robert Kennedy of New York announced that he too would run for president. Kennedy was the younger brother of the recently slain president, and millions of people were simultaneously thrilled at the prospect that another Kennedy might occupy the White House and terrified at the prospect that another Kennedy would be murdered.

And Bobby Kennedy indeed was murdered: on June 5, 1968, just after winning the primary election in California, he was shot and killed as he left the hotel ballroom where he had made a speech celebrating his victory. When he died, some of his supporters began dreaming that the last surviving Kennedy brother, Ted, who was a senator from Massachusetts, would run. Others turned to George McGovern, a senator from South Dakota who, like McCarthy, was fiercely opposed to the war.

By summer, it became clear what the likely outcome would be: McCarthy's campaign was floundering, attracting mostly college students and other young people but not older Democrats. McGovern was having the same problems, compounded by the fact that almost no one had ever heard of him. And Teddy Kennedy, mourning another murder in his family and likely concerned for his own safety, made it clear that he did not want to run. That left Vice President Hubert Humphrey, whom most of the powerful people in the party supported once Johnson pulled out of the race.

Humphrey more or less supported Johnson's policies, which meant he more or less supported Johnson's war, which meant that many more young men would be sent to Vietnam to fight. Many thousands of those young men, and just as many young women, decided that they would not tolerate that. So they would go to Chicago when the Democrats were there and they would make their stand in the parks and in the streets and in front of the International Amphitheater itself. They would demand that if a different candidate could not be chosen, the party would at least promise to change its policies and end the war and stop the dying.

The leaders of the Democrats were not a bit happy about that: political parties like to look organized and unified—like the Republicans were—and thousands of young people protesting in the streets would send the wrong message to the millions of Americans who would be watching the convention on TV. The leaders of Chicago were unhappy too, especially Richard Daley, the gruff, powerful sixty-six-year-old mayor of the city, famous for his toughness, temper and unapologetic taste for the power his job afforded him. Before the convention, Daley arranged for the streets to be patrolled by nearly 12,000 Chicago police, 7,500 army troops and another 7,500 members of the Illinois National Guard. While Daley could not issue orders to the solders or the Guardsmen, he could tell his police exactly what to do. And he was clear about two things: they were to keep the peace and, if they felt they needed to, they were to shoot to kill. The police were armed. The protesters weren't. The young blood that was being spilled in Vietnam might, it seemed, soon be spilled in Chicago too.

If the thousands of delegates and guests arriving in Chicago for the convention hadn't heard otherwise, they'd think the city had no concerns at all about the week to come. The grand boulevards converging on the amphitheater had been lined with banners depicting scenes of nature—birds and flowers mostly—to create a sense more of parkland than of city. Chicago was known for its stockyards—vast pens where cattle and hogs were kept, slaughtered and packed—and while the yards were a Chicago landmark and an important part of the city's economy, they looked bad and smelled worse. For the convention, attractive redwood fences were thus built to conceal them.

Once the delegates got to their hotels and the convention hall, however, the illusion of a city planning a party was broken. Steel fences topped with barbed wire surrounded the amphitheater; the doors to the arena had been fitted with bulletproof glass. The streets around the hotels where the delegates were staying were patrolled by the armed and uniformed police and soldiers. Even the weather was causing problems, with air conditioners struggling to keep up with the heat, and power flickering in elevators and even telephones. What's more, the city's taxi drivers had chosen just that week to go on strike for higher pay—smart from the perspective of the drivers themselves, who were refusing to work just when the city needed them most, but disastrous from the point of view of the convention planners.

On August 25, the night before the convention officially opened, the trouble began. The protesters had tried to get permits to sleep in Lincoln Park so that they could march to the amphitheater during the day, but Daley refused. The protesters camped out there anyway, intending to hold what they called a Festival of Life—singing, dancing, chanting and calling for peace. But no festival—of life or any other kind—had been approved and the police ordered the gathering to disperse. The protesters refused. The police repeated the order and the protesters remained unmoved. A command was thus given, and officers carrying grenade guns fired canisters of tear gas into the crowd, stinging the eyes of the demonstrators and making it impossible for them to see. As they poured from the park, trying to escape the gas, they were pursued by the police—through traffic, down sidewalks and eventually downtown to the hotels where the delegates were staying, including the Conrad Hilton Hotel, where Humphrey and McCarthy and their campaign teams had claimed a large group of rooms.

There were just a few skirmishes and just a few arrests on that first night, but over the next few days, the crowd of demonstrators grew to its expected 10,000. As it did, the tension grew and the confrontations with the police increased. There were more bursts of tear gas, more arrests, and some of the protesters began fighting back, hurling rocks and bottles—potentially deadly weapons if they are thrown fast enough and accurately enough. Some of the police were indeed injured, but the helmets and face shields they wore offered a measure of protection; many of them carried plastic shields as well. The protesters, who had no such equipment, were in much greater danger, especially when they tried to rally at the amphitheater and the police pushed them back—swinging wooden clubs and often drawing blood. The convention delegates saw the coverage of the fighting on TVs in the hall and, later, back in their hotel rooms. Before long, some of that violence crept into the hall as well.

Each state was allowed to send what was called a slate—or a group—of delegates to the convention. The bigger the state, the bigger the slate: Delaware, a small state, got twenty-two delegates; Missouri got sixty; Pennsylvania got a hundred and thirty. In the case of some states, two competing slates showed up. One might be more diverse than another—with more Black people and women included; one might be more in favor of or opposed to the war. Only one slate from each state could be seated.

In the case of Georgia, the competition between the two groups of forty-three delegates began to grow heated, and one delegate was forcibly removed from the hall by security guards—something that was never supposed to happen at an orderly convention. Dan Rather, a thirty-seven-year-old reporter for CBS News, tried to interview the delegate, pushing his way through the crowd with his microphone in hand and a TV camera trailing him. The security guards then turned on him, overpowering him and knocking him to the floor. Throughout, he managed to keep hold of his microphone and continued reporting what was happening, his camera feed going to Walter Cronkite, the grandfatherly CBS anchorman in the broadcast booth.

"Walter," he said, "we tried to talk to the man and we got violently pushed out of the way. This is the kind of thing that has been going on outside the hall; this is the first time we've had it happen inside the hall." He stopped, panting. "I'm sorry to be out of breath, but somebody belted me in the stomach during that."

Cronkite, who had covered many conventions before and did not care to see his younger reporters placed in danger, responded angrily. "I think we've got a bunch of thugs here, Dan," he said.

As disturbing as the brawling both in the amphitheater and on the streets was becoming, things were likely only to get worse the next day, Wednesday, August 28, when the most important business of the convention would begin. Before a political party can officially choose its candidate, it must debate and vote on what is known as a platform, a series of ideas and promises the party would implement if its candidate won. "Platform" was a nice metaphor for what the promises were, since it suggested a foundation of ideals on which the party would stand.

The metaphor went further too: Each plan in the platform was known as a "plank." There would be a plank concerning education, another concerning health care, another concerning civil rights. And in the case of the Democrats in 1968, there was hope that there would be a peace plank—a plan to end the war in Vietnam and bring home the boys who were fighting and dying there. The McCarthy and McGovern forces on the convention floor supported the peace plank; the Humphrey forces did not. There was no question that the debate would be angry, and the way things were already going, quite possibly violent.

The demonstrators in the streets were following the events inside the convention hall, using transistor radios and word of mouth in an age before anyone had ever heard of a smartphone or the internet. The news they were hearing was not good. The Humphrey forces in the hall were powerful, and few people expected the peace plank to pass.

By the middle of the afternoon, the demonstrators were growing discouraged by the news, and a crowd of several thousand had gathered in Grant Park, preparing for speeches and chants at the huge, light blue band shell where outdoor concerts were usually performed. The plan was that after the speeches, they would leave the park and try once more to march the four miles to the amphitheater so that they could be present outside when the peace plank was voted on. Later that night, the delegates would also vote on who the presidential nominee would be—and the demonstrators wanted to be there for that too. If their jeers and chants outside the hall could be heard inside, perhaps the delegates would know that they did not want a candidate like Humphrey, who would only continue the war.

At just after 3:30 p.m., as the speeches were getting underway at the band shell, one demonstrator did something entirely unplanned. Standing at the base of a tall flagpole that was visible throughout the park, he took hold of the rope to which the American flag fluttering at the top was attached. Unspooling the rope, he lowered the flag. No one knew who the demonstrator was. Most people assumed he was just one more student, and the thousands of other demonstrators cheered at what he had done. Others would suspect he was actually working for the police or the city, disguised as a student and told to do something provocative, something that would offend and inflame the police and the National Guardsmen—for whom the flag was a powerful patriotic symbol—and give them a reason to chase the students from the park. Whoever the young man was, the flag drop had precisely that effect—delighting the students and enraging the police, who decided now was the time to act.

Marilyn Katz, a twenty-one-year-old member of the SDS, was there at that moment, and even half a century later remembers vividly what unfolded. "It's hot, it's sunny, the crowd is massive," she said in a *New York Times* interview on the fiftieth anniversary of the demonstrations in 2018. "This phalanx of cops comes into the back of the crowd and is just whaling into the crowd. People are running and getting knocked to the ground."

The police were indiscriminate in whom and how they hit—swinging clubs and striking demonstrators in the head, shoulders and back. The students pushed back and began chanting "Pig, pig, pig," over and over again at the police. They also chanted, *"Sieg Heil!"* a term that means "Hail victory" in German. It was something the Nazis used to cheer at their rallies, never so lustily as when Adolf Hitler was delivering a speech. The police, unsurprisingly, took offense at that and began swinging harder, charging farther, shoving the crowd backward until they came up to a row of old benches with flaking green paint and tumbled over them. Still the police came, advancing over bodies, swinging clubs. The demonstrators responded by picking up more rocks and more bottles and began throwing them.

At the edge of the crowd, some officers raised their grenade guns and fired more tear gas canisters into the crowd. One canister hit the ground before it burst its cap and released its terrible cloud of stinging gas. A demonstrator plucked it up and hurled it back at the police. The crowd cheered; the police pressed in farther.

As the melee spread—with clubs swinging, protesters falling, blood running in the grass and paths of the park—the demonstrators made their way to the exits, battled the police there and broke free. The violence in Grant Park was now certain to spread like a blaze throughout the city.

If any of the demonstrators who were doing battle in the streets had had an opportunity to turn back to their transistor radios, they would have heard that the news from the convention hall was as bad as they feared. The peace plank had lost—and lost by a lot: of more than 2,600 delegates, 1,041 had voted in favor of it and 1,568 voted against. Even while the roll call of the states was still being called and each delegation was casting its votes, it became clear what the outcome would be. In response, the delegations from New York and California staged a demonstration of their own. Together, they made up 362 of the total number of delegates and most of them had favored ending the war. As the *no* votes rolled in, they linked arms and began swaying and singing "We Shall Overcome," a powerful—but also sorrowful—anthem of the civil rights movement.

Mayor Daley and the convention floor managers suspected the New Yorkers and Californians would make just this kind of trouble and had seated them at the back of the hall, hoping that it would be hard for the television cameras, which were mostly positioned near the front, to see them. As the singing began, the floor managers also cut the power to the New York and California microphones. But it was no good: roving reporters were everywhere, accompanied by TV crews with cameras, and everything that went on was thus being shown to the world.

The same was true—on an even greater scale—outside the hall. By now it was evening and the demonstrators who had broken out of Grant Park had battled their way as far as Congress Street, which connected to Michigan Avenue—which itself led to the amphitheater. They were joined by other demonstrators from all over the city. The police tried to cut them off, firing more tear gas, swinging more clubs. Police vans pulled up—each able to hold fifty people. The officers began dragging the bleeding demonstrators out of the crowd and tossing them into the open backs of the vans. As the crowd swarmed ahead, a police officer spotted a TV crew broadcasting the scene and forced the cameraman to turn off his light, plunging the scene into darkness. A newspaper photographer at Michigan Avenue and Van Buren Street waded into the crowd and spotted the police—who didn't want photographs any more than they wanted TV coverage. Sensing the danger, the photographer held his hands over his head and clasped them together, showing that he was carrying no rocks, bottles or other weapons.

"Press! Press!" he shouted. A police officer descended and arrested him anyway. "What did I do? What did I do?" the photographer asked.

"If you don't know, you shouldn't be a photographer," the officer answered, hustling him off to a van.

A Presbyterian chaplain from Yale University who was working with the McCarthy campaign was also arrested when he tried to stop the police from beating a college girl who was one of the protesters. He shouted, "Don't hit a woman!" at the police, but like Dan Rather in the convention floor, he was hit in the stomach, and then he was arrested.

Back in the amphitheater, the delegates, who had moved beyond the vote on the peace plank, were now beginning the process of voting on their presidential candidate. But first each name—Humphrey, McCarthy, McGovern—had to be placed officially in nomination, with a speech by one of their supporters explaining why that person was the right one for the presidency. McGovern's name was introduced by Abraham Ribicoff, a senator from Connecticut. Like most of the other people in the hall, he had seen the TV coverage of what was by now a citywide riot, and like most of those other people, he was horrified by what he saw. He blamed Mayor Daley, who controlled the city and the police and who thus, he believed, should bear the responsibility for the bloodshed.

"With George McGovern as president of the United States," Ribicoff declared in his speech, "we wouldn't have to have Gestapo tactics in the streets of Chicago!"

Once again, someone had invoked the Nazis—this time the regime's murderous secret police. And coming from someone who was Jewish, as Ribicoff was, it carried an extra authority—and an extra sting—since it was Jews the Nazis had killed by the millions during the war. Daley erupted. Sitting in the audience near the front of the hall, he cupped his right hand next to his mouth and shouted up at Ribicoff. No microphone was able to pick up his voice, but lip readers believed they knew just what he said, and that was: "F— you, you Jew son of a b—!" Daley's supporters disputed it, claiming the mayor had shouted only: "You faker!"

Whatever Daley had said, Ribicoff knew he had hit a nerve. "How hard it is to accept the truth," he said.

Many people thought Ribicoff may have gone too far in invoking the Gestapo, but the officers in the Chicago streets were showing no signs of bringing themselves under control. Indeed, they were only escalating the violence, as were the protesters.

A helicopter roared in and hovered overhead, its searchlight playing across the ground, its rotor blades emitting a deafening roar and setting off a storm of wind that caught and spread the tear gas. Demonstrators staggered to fountains and plunged their faces in the water, trying to rinse the gas from their eyes. Those who could still stand and chant did so.

"The streets belong to the people, the streets belong to the people!" they shouted.

A sixteen-year-old demonstrator—the son of diplomats—had

traveled from Michigan to be present for the protests and now, caught in the fighting, he picked up a stray brick. Other demonstrators saw him and began shouting, "Throw it! Throw it!" Pulled in one direction by everything he had ever been taught about obeying the law, and in the other by the fury of the crowd and the passion of its cause, he froze. "Throw it! Throw it!" the demonstrators continued. Finally he did throw it, hurling the brick through the nearby window of a bank.

The worst of the fighting was now centered around the Conrad Hilton Hotel, with demonstrators converging on the place they knew Humphrey and McCarthy were staying—but not everyone in the swarm around the building was involved in the fighting. Directly in front of the hotel, a few dozen people were simply watching the demonstrations, standing behind security barricades that had been set up by police, believing they'd be safe there. But wordlessly and inexplicably, the police turned on them.

The helmeted line advanced on them with their clubs raised. The group behind the barricades, terrified, began backing toward the hotel. The police advanced farther, and the bystanders retreated farther and were ultimately pressed up against the giant plate-glass window of the hotel's restaurant, the Haymarket Inn. Some of the trapped people tried to squirm out sideways, but they could not move; others tried to push back against the police, but the police were too strong, pressing them harder and harder against the glass. Inside the restaurant, diners watched in horror, backing away from the window as it became clear what was going to happen. Finally, inevitably, it did happen, as the window smashed and the crowd tumbled through it in a spray of sharp glass shards. The police swarmed through and began beating the bystanders where they fell.

High above, on the fifteenth floor of the hotel, where McCarthy's campaign headquarters were located, volunteers had set up a makeshift hospital, where they brought battered protesters and bandaged their wounds. Ten floors higher, on the twenty-fifth, the Humphrey team had set up its own camp. There were no demonstrators here, there was no first aid being administered. There was only an organized team of aides and volunteers preparing for what they expected to be the formal selection of their candidate as the Democratic nominee for president of the United States. In his own suite, Humphrey tried to focus on the evening ahead, but even so high up in the Hilton tower, he could smell and feel the sting of the tear gas.

Down in the street, the protesters, mindful of the TV cameras that were everywhere, began chanting at the police, "The whole world is watching! The whole world is watching!" And the whole world was.

Long before the last of the blood had been hosed from the streets and the last of the demonstrators had either been arrested or chased off, the events marched ahead in the convention hall as planned. Humphrey, as everyone expected, was chosen as the nominee, winning easily, with 1,762 votes to 601 for McCarthy and just 147 for McGovern. Humphrey chose Edmund Muskie—a reasonable, agreeable and, to voters, very appealing senator from Maine as his vice presidential running mate. But that would help him little. The country had watched what happened when the Democrats held their convention and decided that a party that could not be trusted to conduct a four-day meeting without descending into chaos surely could not be trusted to run a nation.

It was not an entirely fair conclusion. The delegates in the hall were by no means responsible for the demonstrators and police throughout in the city, but elections are won and lost as much on impressions voters have of the candidates and parties as on anything else. Three months later, on November 5, the Republicans' Richard Nixon would be elected president, with his running mate, Maryland governor Spiro Agnew, becoming vice president.

Johnson's war would quickly become Nixon's war, and never mind a speedy peace; the fighting and dying in Vietnam would go on for seven more years, until the last of the Americans finally left the country in 1975. In 1968, the year that the protesters had hoped the war would stop, 16,899 American boys would die. In 1969, another 11,780 were killed. Ultimately, 58,220 Americans lost their lives in the war. No one knows exactly how many Vietnamese died, but some estimates put the total at a staggering 2 million civilians and 1.1 million soldiers. The North Vietnamese nonetheless achieved their goals—driving the Americans out of their country and ending their civil war under a communist government.

More than 650 of the demonstrators in Chicago were arrested in the fighting; most of them were charged with relatively minor crimes like disorderly conduct and were quickly released. Close to 200 police officers were injured. An official investigation in the months that followed would largely—but not entirely—absolve the demonstrators of blame for the violence in Chicago. They were outnumbered and unarmed and untrained for street violence. The officers were supposed to be the ones who had the training and equipment to keep the peace, not engage in the fighting. Indeed, the report would stingingly label the violence "a police riot," one that "was made all the more shocking by the fact that it was often inflicted upon persons who had broken no law, disobeyed no order, made no threat."

The anti-war movement went on after Chicago, and the demonstrations grew far larger and more coordinated. In November 1969, half a million people gathered in Washington, D.C., demanding an end to the fighting. In 1971, huge demonstrations were held on both coasts, with 200,000 people returning to Washington and 165,000 gathering in San Francisco. All across the country, other anti-war demonstrations broke out on campuses, some peaceful, some less so. In May 1970, the very worst possible consequence of the unrest occurred on the campus of Kent State University in Ohio, when National Guardsmen opened fire on protesters, killing four students.

Slowly, painfully, lessons were learned. There was no way of avoiding the reality that occasionally—sometimes more than occasionally—demonstrators and police would face off on opposite sides of a security divide. In a democracy like America's, that was inevitable, especially since the Constitution itself guarantees the freedom of assembly. But both police and demonstrators could agree that nobody wanted another Kent State, nobody wanted another Chicago. Social justice movements advance haltingly, sometimes sloppily, but the hope—ever and always—is that they can do so peacefully too.

The Stonewall Inn, as it appeared in 1969.

SEVEN

The Stonewall Uprising
1969

IF YOU LIVED in New York City in 1969 and you had a choice, you'd be awfully unlikely to pick the bar called the Stonewall Inn on Christopher Street as a place to go drinking and dancing. Christopher Street itself was lovely—a pretty little stretch in the lower Manhattan neighborhood of Greenwich Village, where the random mix of crooked blocks was so much more old-world than the strict street grid of most of Manhattan. Just across the street from the Stonewall was the small triangular patch of Christopher Park, and just around the corner was the smaller still, quainter still Sheridan Square.

But all that charm was only on the outside. Inside Stonewall, things were less pleasant. There was no plumbing behind the bar, so glasses were simply rinsed in a tub of water, dried off and set out to be used again. The bathrooms did have plumbing—but only barely—and when the sinks and toilets weren't overflowing, they often just broke down completely. There were no emergency exits in the inn, meaning that in the event of a fire, the customers and employees would likely be trapped. The drinks were overpriced and watered down, diluted so that customers would order more—and pay more—and the owners could make a single bottle last longer.

And then there was the matter of the police. Once a month at least, the inn would be raided. The colorful swirl of lights on the dance floor would suddenly go off, the bright white overhead lights would go on and the police officers would line all of the customers up against the wall, check their identification, arrest some of them, let the others go and confiscate the bottles of liquor behind the bar. The people who were arrested were typically the ones who had violated the city's laws against dressing in clothing associated with another gender.

A man who dressed entirely in women's clothing was someone the lawmakers and psychologists called a transvestite or a cross-dresser and the gay community at the time called a drag queen. Today we have a much better grasp of gender identity. In the 1960s, no one used the word "transgender," mostly because there was little understanding by government officials or medical professionals that plenty of people who are assigned one biological sex identify as another one. However, some people who identified as drag queens at that time would now be identified as transgender, and others as gender nonconforming—those who exhibit behaviors or traits that do not conform to expectations of gender expression. Today the term "drag queen" is used to describe performance artists who dramatize gender.

Often drag queens at the Stonewall were easy enough for the police to spot. But other cases of gay men or lesbian women borrowing a coat or sweater or shirt or blouse were harder to define and criminalize, so the law made things simple: a person who was not wearing at least three articles of so-called gender-appropriate clothing would be subject to arrest. In the event the clothing was so ambiguous that it was hard to tell exactly what physical anatomy the wearer had, the policemen would always show up with a few police women, who would escort the suspect to a bathroom and conduct a physical examination. That may have settled the matter one way or the other, but it both humiliated and violated the person who was subjected to it.

The people who were arrested at the Stonewall for wearing what the law considered the wrong clothes would be taken—or sometimes dragged—out of the bar in custody, sometimes walking directly into a crush of onlookers who had gathered on the street. Often reporters from New York's newspapers were there too. The *Village Voice*, a small weekly paper that, as its name suggested, served mostly Greenwich Village, was located directly across the street, and its reporters were no friends of the gay community. They would not use the word "gay" in their pages— except in advertisements for apartments that included the line "No gays allowed." They had no hesitation, however, about using other words in their stories—words meant to cut and to hurt, like "fag" or "queer" or "fairy." Flinging ugly names at gay men also served to oppress them further, in the same way that ugly racial terms were meant to keep Black people apart from—and beneath—white people.

Reporters from the more mainstream *New York Times*, *New York Post* and *New York Daily News* would generally avoid the ugly language but might show up for the raids as well, alerted by police radios that they kept with them to stay abreast of crimes or arrests as they occurred. The next day, the names and even the faces of the people who had been arrested would appear in the paper—in many cases exposing a secret that they had been forced to spend their whole lives trying to keep.

When the raid at last was over, the bright lights in the Stonewall would go back off, the colorful lights would go back on and the shaken customers who hadn't been arrested would try to put the latest scare out of their minds and resume their evening. The bar owners helped: they were, by now, so accustomed to police raids that they kept an extra supply of liquor bottles hidden away so that they could resume business as soon as the police left.

With all that, it made no sense at all to come to the Stonewall, especially with a choice of 10,000 other bars and dance clubs in New York City. But the thing was, the gay and lesbian patrons who made up the Stonewall's clientele didn't have that choice—not if the reason they were going to the bar in the first place was to mingle and dance and maybe meet a partner and fall in love.

The government of New York City, like the rest of the country, had some very clear ideas about what would later be called LGBTQ+ people. For starters, they thought they had a mental illness. A federal study in the 1950s had reached that conclusion, saying: "It is generally believed that those who engage in overt acts of perversion lack the emotional stability of normal persons." A safety film shown to schoolchildren went further, warning boys especially to stay away from "the homosexual" because gay men suffer from "a sickness that [is] not visible like smallpox, but is no less dangerous and contagious: a sickness of the mind."

It wasn't just the government or the school boards that believed that; the doctors themselves agreed. The 1952 edition of the *Diagnostic and Statistical Manual*—the guide psychologists and psychiatrists use to define and treat mental illness—listed homosexuality as a "sociopathic personality disturbance." The second edition, published in 1968, used milder but no less negative language, calling same-sex attraction a "sexual deviation."

"Sexual deviants" were not the kinds of people the city officials wanted to see gathering in one place at one time, especially if drinking and dancing were involved. New York had a tidy way to prevent that from happening. Bars could not operate without a liquor license, and it was up to the State Liquor Authority (SLA) to grant or deny them. The SLA didn't want to grant licenses to establishments where patrons were regularly disorderly—getting into fights, disturbing the neighborhood, endangering the public. It was a simple matter then to declare that any gathering of gay men or lesbian women was, by definition, disorderly—no matter how they actually behaved—so the license would be refused.

Gay bars still operated—on the sly and in the shadows, like the Stonewall Inn. The police knew they were there and would raid them now and then as the law required. But the police didn't want the bars to close altogether, because many of the officers had arrangements with the owners: they would warn them in advance of a raid and would conduct it early in the evening so that the bar could resume its evening's business and unpack its fresh bottles from their secret location. In exchange, the police would receive a monthly envelope of cash.

So the police still came and the gay patrons still came—despite the dirty glasses and the miserable drinks and the threat of arrest and public humiliation—because the bars were places the customers felt welcome, places they weren't judged. And they came to the Stonewall most of all. Drag queens were often seen as too flamboyant by gay men who were hoping to be as inconspicuous as possible, but the Stonewall opened its doors to them. Transgender people were often shunned too. But the Stonewall opened its doors to them as well. It even welcomed homeless gay people, who were often as not teenage boys who'd been rejected by their families and had moved to New York because they knew there was a gay community there. Many of the boys made their home on a patch of grass in Christopher Park, hoping to raise just enough by panhandling to pay the three-dollar admission the Stonewall charged, which would mean an evening indoors, out of the weather and away from the shame and social exclusion they felt everywhere.

It was a lonely arrangement—an entire community of people who felt at home in just one bar out of all the others in the city—but the gay, lesbian, transgender and gender-nonconforming customers who came to the Stonewall accepted that it was the best arrangement they would get. And then, finally, in the just-after-midnight hours of June 28, 1969—a sweltering day in a year in which demonstrations in favor of civil rights and against the war in Vietnam had made it clear that social change was coming—the door of the Stonewall once again burst open, the colorful lights on the dance floor once again went off and the bright lights overhead once again went on. But this time something would be different. This time the people in the bar would not accept that they weren't entitled to want something more. And they would decide that they were ready to fight for it.

For anyone paying attention, it was clear that things could not go on much longer before tempers blew. The push for gay rights had been slowly gaining momentum for nearly twenty years. In 1950, Los Angeles–area gay men created a group called the Mattachine Society—named after the Société Mattachine, a medieval troupe of male performers who traveled from village to village, putting on shows that satirized, and thus exposed, social injustice. The modern-day Mattachines would expose social injustice too, but they would do so in a much less colorful way. Gay men were often dismissed as loud and flamboyant, so the Mattachines would push back against that, demonstrating for their rights politely, seeking to prove that gay people could assimilate quietly, almost inconspicuously. Shortly after, a similar group, the Daughters of Bilitis—named after the fictional author of an 1894 collection of erotic poetry—was founded to pursue similar rights and acceptance for lesbians.

But good manners weren't working, especially in the 1960s, when, in New York at least, things seemed only to be getting worse. In 1964, the city was set to host the World's Fair, with tens of millions of people from all over the planet visiting the fairgrounds in the borough of Queens.

It would not do for those guests to encounter the unseemly crowds at the city's not-so-secret gay bars. Mayor Robert Wagner thus ordered a crackdown. The raids would not be occasional or gentle—the police would come more frequently, arrest more people and force more gay, lesbian and transgender people into the glare of public humiliation.

Even after the fair closed, the pressure on the gay community continued, with raids at all the clubs growing in frequency and ferocity. By June 1969, many of the bars had been shut down completely. The Stonewall pressed on, but was increasingly feeling endangered too. On June 24—a Tuesday night, which was typically a quiet night—the bar was raided. If the officers were starting to show up during the week, they'd surely be back on the weekend. And they were.

The first sign of trouble came quietly—even invisibly. In the crush of customers late that Friday evening, a pair of men and a pair of women wandered in, paid their three-dollar cover charge and mingled inconspicuously with the crowd. It was likely no one noticed that they drank no alcohol. It was likely too that no one noticed that they did not appear to know any of the other customers, talking mostly among themselves. They scanned the room, as if they were looking for friends they were supposed to meet—but no such friends appeared. What the two men and two women were doing instead was studying the room and the clientele. They could estimate how many people were there—at least 200 and perhaps a few more. They could guess at which of the people were violating the three-articles-of-clothing rule, but could not confirm their suspicions without the humiliation of the bathroom body check.

All four of the new arrivals were carrying badges in their pockets that identified them as members of the Public Morals Squad—the arm of the police department that was assigned the job of preventing homosexual people from gathering and engaging in behavior that was only permitted between men and women. Sometime after midnight, one of the four made his way to the wall near the restrooms where the Stonewall's pay phone was. He dropped in a dime, dialed a number, and a phone rang in the police department's nearby Sixth Precinct station house. The phone was answered, a few words were exchanged and the familiar machinery of a raid was engaged.

At 1:20 a.m., that raid began, when the front door of the Stonewall banged open and five more police officers burst in. "Police!" one of them shouted to the startled patrons. "We're taking the place!"

Immediately, the bartender obeyed the rules of the raid, turning the dance lights off, turning the white lights on, stopping the music—but he was confused. It was too late in the evening for a raid to begin, and the usual warning call had not come in advance. This time it was not a just-for-show raid; this time, the police clearly meant business.

"Against the wall, against the wall!" one of them commanded. "Identification!"

Several of the customers who had experience with Stonewall raids bolted in the direction of the bathrooms, where there were small windows leading to the safety of the streets. But the police officers who had the same experience stood in their path and pushed them back to the dance floor.

"Against the wall!" the police said. "Now!"

The customers retreated from the dance floor and tried to line the walls as they'd been ordered, but there were too many of them trying to move through too small a space and several of them slowed or stumbled. The police advanced and shoved them backward.

"Identification!" the police officers repeated. The crackle of the walkie-talkies the officers carried on their belts sounded through the bar.

The customers did as they were told, presenting their driver's licenses if they had them, and their library cards, social security cards or student identification cards if they didn't. Many of them also presented their draft cards. With the war in Vietnam still raging, men nineteen years old or over could be ordered into the army and sent to the other side of the world to do battle in the Southeast Asian jungles. They were forbidden to dance at home; yet they could be commanded to fight overseas.

The police now moved along the line, checking the identification cards, comparing faces to photos and asking the underage boys where they lived and what they were doing in a bar at all. The customers were all behaving as they had before—cooperatively, submissively— but then all at once they weren't. A few of the ones who were pulled forward wrenched free and refused to accompany the policewomen to the bathrooms. A few who had already been examined, had failed the body test and had been placed under arrest refused orders to move toward the door to be loaded into a police van outside. Everyone in the line whose identities had not yet been checked put their ID cards away and looked defiantly at the police.

The nine officers looked back at the 200 or more customers—and at that moment, a subtle shift took place in the room. The officers had the law on their side. The customers had the numbers on theirs. And the customers had something else too, something less tangible: they had pain on their side, they had grievance on their side, they had years of enduring the ugly names on their side. They had been chased out of their communities, out of their homes, out of the other clubs and bars where they used to meet, to this one place on this one street in this one New York neighborhood. And they'd well and truly had enough.

The officers may have sensed that or may have not, but either way, they decided that their best and safest course was to empty the entire bar fast, before a brawl broke out in the cramped space. They ordered everyone outside—but again they were defied. Some of the people stayed where they were, glaring back at the police with the same icy, immovable look. Some of the men did obey and left the bar, but they did not scatter as they normally would have—grateful to have avoided arrest and hoping only to disappear as quickly as possible. Instead they remained on the street, where bystanders and passersby began to join them. A crowd of 150 or so people filled the sidewalk and flowed out to Christopher Street.

Someone took up a chant. "Gay power!" he shouted, raising an arm and pumping a fist.

"Liberate the bar!" a voice responded.

A third person then answered them both, choosing one of the words that had been used to shame gay people but now would serve as a statement of defiance—a word wielded like a thrown stone. "Fag power!" he shouted. At that, the crowd whooped and cheered.

Drawn by the noise and the flashing lights of the parked police cars, still more people began to congregate, with the crowd growing to 200, then 300, then 400. The nine officers and a few dozen Stonewall customers were still inside, and at this point the police determined that they couldn't leave. The vans that would be used to take away the people who had been arrested had not yet arrived. If the police came outside now, they'd only incite violence. Instead, they slammed the door of the bar and locked it. The officers who had come to arrest the patrons were now themselves imprisoned with some of the customers who had not made it out, barricaded inside as the mob and the anger continued to grow outside.

As more people shouted, *"Gay power,"* others began singing "We Shall Overcome," the same song crowds had sung during the March on Washington six years earlier and at the Democratic Convention in Chicago the summer before. The officers inside frantically radioed for the vans, and at last they arrived, creeping along Christopher Street with their sirens wailing and their lights flashing, nudging aside the protesters who were in their path. When they had come to a stop, the door of the bar cracked open and the police inside emerged, shoving the men and women they planned to arrest ahead of them.

The crowd began booing and jeering. A few shouted, "Pigs!" at the police, another echo of the previous summer's violence in Chicago. A rumor had begun to circulate that the bar was raided because the police had not received their usual envelopes of cash, and someone called, "Let's pay them off!" At that, handfuls of coins were flung at the police, pinging off the vans and cars and scattering in the streets.

Moving faster now, the officers began to shove the cross-dressed patrons into the open backs of the vans. Some went inside without trouble; others squirmed away and broke free—to more cheers from the crowd. Finally, one police officer emerged from the bar with one of the few woman customers in tow. She was fighting furiously—hitting, kicking, cursing and squirming. Her name was Stormé DeLarverie, and she had once been part of a stage troupe called the Jewel Box Revue. She would perform dressed as a man, and she was dressed that way tonight.

"Move along, faggot!" the officer grunted, speaking to her as if she were indeed a man. The word was ugly no matter who was its target, and she began to fight harder. At that, he raised his wooden baton and hit her across the head. She responded by punching him in the face; then she looked out at the crowd of people watching.

"Why don't you guys do something?" she shouted just as the officer tossed her into the back of the van.

At that, the contained violence turned into open violence. Perhaps it was the sight of an unarmed person being struck by an armed one. Perhaps it was the challenge DeLaverie's question posed—*Why don't you guys do something?* Whatever it was, the crowd snapped. Someone threw a can; someone else threw a bottle. Someone picked up a cobblestone, threw it in rage, and it struck one of the Stonewall's windows. The windows were covered in plywood inside to ensure privacy and protect against damage during raids, but the glass on the outside smashed and the plywood cracked.

More bottles and cans and cobblestones now flew, and the crowd began to scream and curse and advance on the building. The police and customers who had not climbed aboard the vans retreated inside and once more slammed and locked the door, along with a reporter from the *Village Voice* named Howard Smith, who had forced his way through the melee. Inside, the walls shook as the cobblestones struck the building, smashing more windows. Bricks from a nearby construction site followed, along with a heavy metal trash can, which crashed into the door.

"Aren't you guys scared?" Smith asked the police.

"No," they answered, but he didn't believe them. They looked terrified.

At the curb, several of the demonstrators took hold of a parking meter and began yanking it violently from side to side until the concrete of the sidewalk around its base cracked and they pulled it free. They held it in front of them like a battering ram and ran at the Stonewall door, pounding it again and again and causing it to shake in its frame. One of the officers inside unholstered his gun, pointed it at the closed door and shouted:

"Get away from there or I'll shoot!"

The pounding stopped briefly but then resumed. Another officer armed himself with a baseball bat kept behind the bar, and yet another grabbed his gun. "We'll shoot the first one that comes through the door!" he yelled.

Finally, the door gave way and the police pushed back against it as the crowd tried to force its way in. One of the officers found a fire hose behind the bar and pointed it out the door while another turned on the water. But while fire hoses had knocked civil rights protesters off their feet and into walls in the streets of Montgomery, Alabama, six summers before, this one could produce only a weak spray that did little more than wet the sidewalk and cause some of the protesters to slip. The police were able to slam and bolt the door once more, but worse was coming.

Most of the Stonewall crowd did not want to destroy the very bar that they were trying to defend. And most of them did not want to hurt—much less kill—the officers and other patrons trapped inside. But the few caught up in the heat of their rage did not care.

At one of the spots in one of the windows where the plywood had cracked, a hand from outside was thrust inside holding a small can; the can sprayed a liquid that had the sharp, petroleum smell of lighter fluid. The hand withdrew and then reappeared, this time with a lit match. The match was tossed and the lighter fluid burst into flame. One of the patrons still inside sprayed lighter fluid on the surface of the bar itself and that flared too. The fires burned only briefly, as the hose—which could not do much to disperse the crowd—at least succeeded in controlling and then extinguishing the flames.

Finally, a half dozen police cars pulled up with their sirens wailing. The officers leapt out, swinging their wooden batons and wading into the crowd. The protesters ducked the blows as best they could and scattered through Christopher Park and up nearby Grove and 4th Streets. But no sooner were they out of harm's way than they doubled back and returned to the site of the Stonewall. Some of them chased the police who had been chasing them—their sheer numbers more powerful than a single officer's baton. Others turned on the police cars, tipping one of them over.

Still more police now arrived—these from the Tactical Patrol Force (TPF), a specialized group trained to break up riots. They formed a wedge, linking arms, and pushed slowly through the crowd, clearing a narrow space, then a wider space, knowing that the energy of a mob feeds on the closeness of the bodies. Wrench them apart, allow in some air, and a blind fury can cool.

The TPF police at last made their way to the door of the Stonewall. The people inside opened it up and the trapped officers were escorted safely to the police cars. They were surely grateful, surely relieved for their rescue. And yet, having escaped with their lives, having escaped uninjured, having witnessed the rage born of pain that had been loosed in the crowd that night—having been in the thick of all that—they still forced thirteen people who had been trapped in the bar with them into the vans. They were, after all that, still under arrest, still to be detained and punished for the crime of wearing the "wrong" clothes, of loving the "wrong" sex.

The sun rose on Saturday morning on a broken-looking Christopher Street. Bottles and bricks and cans and glass and scattered coins lay everywhere. The parking meter that had been used as a battering ram rested where it was dropped; the hurled trash cans lay bent and discarded. The smell of smoke and the stink of lighter fluid hung in the air around the Stonewall.

Before the day was out, the windows of the wrecked inn would be re-boarded, as if the place were closed for good. But soon, three defiant words would be chalked on the fresh plywood: WE ARE OPEN.

The Stonewall did open that night as promised—and there were more protests, more clashes with the police. Scattered confrontations continued on Sunday and again on Monday and Tuesday, though by then a summer rain had come, easing tempers and driving people inside. All the same, it was clear that something had forever changed.

On Sunday, Allen Ginsberg, the openly gay, forty-three-year-old poet who made his home in the neighborhood and had witnessed the riot, spoke to a different *Village Voice* writer. "You know, the guys there were so beautiful," he said. "They've lost that wounded look the fags all had ten years ago."

A neighborhood resident who had been out walking his dog when the fighting broke out described his surprise at what he had seen. "This never, ever happened," he said. "The fairies were not supposed to riot."

But the people of Stonewall did riot—and they did something more important too: they organized. Before the year was out, they formed the Gay Liberation Front—named after the Vietnamese guerilla fighters known as the National Liberation Front—and the Gay Activists Alliance. The groups were founded in New York City, but quickly, new chapters and new groups began appearing around the nation. When 1969 began, there were perhaps fifty gay rights organizations in the United States. By 1971, that total had leapt to 2,500. Gay pride marches were held in 1970—on the anniversary of the first Stonewall riot—in New York, Los Angeles and Chicago, and the following year they spread across the country and then the world, especially to Canada and Western Europe.

Gay men and women took back the language too: protests in front of the *Village Voice* would result in the paper's dropping its terms of disparagement and adopting the word "gay" in its stories. The hate-speech words would be flipped on their heads: The gay community would embrace and claim the word "queer," eventually founding another rights group called Queer Nation. Today the word is used to describe more or less any gender identity or sexuality that does not fit the formal male-female or heterosexual definitions. The word "fag" would, over time, be chased from the language—often referred to as only "the f-word" in the same way racist language is acknowledged just by its first letter so as to deny the word its poison.

Like Black people and women and Jews and Asians and other oppressed groups, the gay community would discover that simply rising up and demanding rights would not be enough. There would be pushback, resistance, hate crimes, ostracism. But the sunlight of openness—of gay pride instead of gay shame—would slowly begin to disinfect that.

In 1973, the *Diagnostic and Statistical Manual* would remove homosexuality from its list of mental illnesses. In 1982, a law preventing workplace discrimination based on sexual orientation would be passed in Wisconsin, and other states would follow. In 2003, the United States Supreme Court would rule that any laws that punished or prohibited consensual sexual acts between same-sex adults were unconstitutional. In 2015, after more and more states began legalizing same-sex marriage, the court declared it legal everywhere in America.

The Stonewall Inn closed and reopened multiple times over the decades—once as a Chinese restaurant, once as a bagel shop. In the 1990s, it reopened as a gay club, closed again in 2006, and opened yet again in 2007, fully renovated. It was designated a New York City landmark in 2015, and in 2017, President Barack Obama declared the inn and the nearly eight-acre site around it a national monument.

In his 2013 inaugural address, Obama elevated Stonewall to its rightful place in the long American march for human rights. The ideal of equality, he said, guides us all, "just as it guided our forebears through Seneca Falls and Selma and Stonewall." With that one line, the riot on that sweltering night in New York City in 1969 joined a list that also included the first declaration of women's rights, signed in 1848, and the march across the Edmund Pettus Bridge in Selma,

Alabama, in 1965, in which Black people pressed ahead despite beatings by the state police.

"Our journey is not complete until our gay brothers and sisters are treated like anyone else under the law," Obama went on, "for if we are truly created equal, then surely the love we commit to one another must be equal as well."

Things aren't quite equal, not just yet. But Obama was right that we are, all of us, on a journey. We have not eradicated hatred and discrimination, but we are making progress, drawing closer. Like the Stonewall Inn itself on the morning after that first night of fighting, a loving America is—and will remain—open.

A Girl Scout picking trash from the Potomac River during the first Earth Day.

EIGHT

Earth Day
1970

RIVERS AREN'T SUPPOSED to catch on fire—and that makes sense. Rivers are made of water; fire and water don't get along, and it's the water that always wins. But nobody ever reckoned with the Cuyahoga River in Ohio, a seemingly unremarkable, eighty-five-mile stretch that winds through the northern part of the state, flows past Cleveland and then empties into Lake Erie. The Cuyahoga was not a river that ever seemed destined to make much news, but in 1969 it did, when, on a pleasant summer Sunday, it suddenly, surreally, burst into flames. It was a scene both horrifying and darkly fanciful—a glimpse into an alternative world in which rivers run foul and water does burn, blotting out the sun with oily black smoke.

But it wasn't an alternative world. It was the world the Earth was becoming—and it was a glimpse of the future that would help rouse the conscience of a nation.

For most of the 12,000 years the Cuyahoga River has cut through its small stretch of the North American landmass, fire was hardly a danger. The river was formed during the last great ice age, as the glaciers retreated and melted, pouring clean, cold Arctic water onto the surrounding land. A new riverway on the old continent was a natural habitat for wildlife, and dozens of species of fish called the Cuyahoga home. Insects and water birds and even bald eagles nested and roosted and skittered across the shoreline and in the trees.

In 1796, Moses Cleaveland, a lawyer and Revolutionary War veteran, was sent by a Connecticut land company to survey the unsettled frontier just west of the fourteen eastern states. When Cleaveland first saw the little river in Ohio, he was struck by its potential to provide both easy access to shipping routes throughout the northern part of the continent and a fertile, resource-rich shoreline that would make it a natural home for future settlers—even if those settlers would take the land of the Iroquois and Algonquian people who already lived there. Cleaveland kept the existing Cuyahoga name—which meant "crooked river" in the Iroquois tongue. He was not so modest when it came to naming the entire region he had surveyed, officially calling it Cleaveland. The name stuck, more or less, though over time the first *a* dropped out. When the settlers did arrive and a new city was born, the editor of a prominent local newspaper wanted to call his publication the *Cleaveland Advertiser*, only he found he could not fit all of the letters on the front-page banner. So Cleaveland became Cleveland and would forever be known that way.

Either way, the young, industrial city soon became great—and then, by the latter half of the nineteenth century, not so great. The problem was that Cleveland was getting filthy, and the Cuyahoga River was perhaps the filthiest part of it. Factories and steel mills grew up along its banks, which made it easy to ship out the goods that were manufactured there, and also provided for a convenient place to dump industrial waste. Why cart off or clean up the chemicals, sludge, animal waste and other muck produced by the manufacturing process when you could just pour them into the river, which would carry them away to Lake Erie, where you'd never see them again?

That actually worked—a very little bit for a very little while. But a growing Cleveland meant a growing waste problem and the river was soon overwhelmed. Among the worst of the waste was oil, which would float on the surface of the water and soak into wood, paper and other trash that was accumulating there too. Collect that much flammable oil in that huge of an expanse and all it would take would be a single match or spark to set off a blaze.

In 1868, just seventy-two years after Moses Cleaveland discovered the clean stretch of wilderness fed by the clear Arctic water, the river did catch fire, likely caused by a steamboat captain who shoveled burnt coal overboard and did not notice—or did not care—that there were still glowing embers mixed in with the ash. It was a sight like none the locals had ever seen before—a river of fire, a vision of hell—but they'd see it again. The Cuyahoga would ignite a dozen times over the next eighty-five years, with the deadliest blaze occurring in 1912, killing five people. The most extensive—and expensive—one happened in 1952, causing $1.3 million in damage to properties along the shore.

By 1968, the entire stretch of river running through the city was a chocolatey, oily brown, with bubbles filled with foul-smelling gasses rising through the filth and breaking the surface. Reporters from *Time* magazine came to visit and were appalled at what they saw.

"It oozes rather than flows," the reporters wrote. "Each day for the past month, 25 million gallons of raw sewage have cascaded from a ruptured pipe, spilling a gray-green torrent into the Cuyahoga." The reporters quoted a mordant joke that locals would tell about the river: "Anyone who falls into the Cuyahoga does not drown, he decays." And they quoted too a report from the federal government on the health of the river. "The lower Cuyahoga has no visible life, not even leeches and sludge worms that usually thrive on wastes."

Then, on June 22, 1969, the seething Cuyahoga erupted once more. It was just past noon when a train passing on an overhead trestle near the Republic Steel mill gave off a spark that fell into the mess below. The river responded the way it had done a dozen times before, which is to say it flashed into flames, with the fire this time rising five stories high and destroying the trestle and a bridge above it. The blaze lasted less than half an hour—Clevelanders had gotten used to the Cuyahoga burning by now and had gotten good at putting out its fires.

Yet something was different this time. The fire might have been just one more incident in the long, sad life of a now-dead river, but it was, at last, one incident too many. For once, the city took notice—the nation took notice. Something was broken; something was diseased in a land that could turn its waterways into sewers, its countryside into wasteland.

Carl Stokes, the mayor of Cleveland, marched to the river the next day and held a press conference in which he demanded change. Stokes was the first Black mayor of a major American city and very much a newsmaker, especially when he was dealing with an emergency in his troubled community. The national press picked up the story of what had happened on the Cuyahoga, Congress picked up on what the national press was reporting, and all over the United States— including on college campuses and in major cities, where people were already mobilized to march against the war in Vietnam and in favor of civil rights—the pulse of civic activism began to quicken again. The war was killing soldiers and civilians, discrimination and prejudice were crushing an entire race of people—and those deaths and that oppression were terrible enough. But a dying environment threatened the entire human species—and all the other species that populate the planet. Something would have to give—and before long, something did.

. . .

The Cuyahoga River was hardly the only part of the United States that was being slowly turned to poison in 1969. Before the year was even a month old, the environmental calamities began.

On January 28, an oil platform six miles off the coast of California was drilling through the ocean floor 3,500 feet deep and ripped open a buried reservoir of thick black oil. Within minutes, the oil began rising to the surface, creating a foul-smelling black slick. The oil poured out at a rate of tens of thousands of gallons a day before being brought more or less under control eleven days later, but by then it was too late: three million gallons had been spilled, leading to an oil slick that extended thirty-five miles. Thousands of sea birds were killed, along with uncounted fish, seals, sea lions, dolphins and more. One dolphin that washed ashore had suffocated—the blowhole on the top of its head through which it breathed had been clogged by oil. The slick was so thick that when the oozing black tide rolled ashore in the evening, it did so without sound—the crash of healthy waves replaced by the heavy silence of sludge.

President Richard Nixon, who had taken office just eight days before the spill and was not known as someone who thought terribly much about the environment, flew from Washington to visit the site of the spill and seemed moved by what he saw. "It is sad that it was necessary that Santa Barbara should be the example that had to bring [ocean pollution] to the attention of the American people," he said. "The Santa Barbara incident has frankly touched the conscience of the American people."

Frank Hartley, the president of Union Oil, the company responsible for the spill, was not nearly so moved. "I don't like to call it a disaster because there has been no loss of human life," he said dismissively. "I am amazed at the publicity for the loss of a few birds."

Hartley's indifference was mirrored by many of the leaders of the other industries that were causing so many of the problems. While covering the Cuyahoga disaster, *Time* dispatched its reporters around the country to learn the state of America's other waterways, and the story that ran in the magazine's August 1, 1969, issue marked the first time many Americans learned the full scope of the environmental mess. In Omaha, the banks of the Missouri River were lined with meatpacking factories, and balls of animal grease the size of oranges were routinely being dumped directly into the water. In Washington, D.C., eighty million gallons of raw sewage were poured into the Potomac River every day. New England's Merrimack River, Pittsburgh's Monongahela, New York's Niagara and Hudson, Alabama and Georgia's Chattahoochee, all ran and bubbled with toxic goo dumped by the factories that had helped build the regions and now were killing them.

All five of the Great Lakes—Huron, Ontario, Michigan, Erie and Superior—were dying too, but it may have been Erie that was suffering the worst. Car, steel and paper manufacturers all poured their wastes into their local waterways, which drained into the lake. Fifty-nine of the sixty-two beaches that were once open for swimming had been closed because they were unsafe. The sludge worms that couldn't survive in the Cuyahoga did thrive in Lake Erie, and with all other aquatic life gone, they had the place to themselves and took advantage of that fact. Every square yard of lake bottom that scientists surveyed was home to as many as 30,000 of the small, slippery animals.

It wasn't just the lakes and rivers that were dying. Americans drove huge cars with oversized engines and filled their tanks with gasoline that contained lead, a toxic metal. The lead made car engines run more smoothly, which was fine, but it also became part of the poisonous exhaust that poured out of the cars' tailpipes after the gas was burned. With tens of millions of cars on tens of thousands of miles of highway, American cities were soon choking under clouds of what looked like a foul combination of smoke and fog—and was thus dubbed smog. No city suffered worse than Los Angeles, which was entirely dependent on cars, got little rain to clear the air and was built in a basin that prevented winds from helping to carry off the heavy brown clouds.

Industrial cities less dependent on cars did not escape similar problems. In Pittsburgh—where the furnaces in steel plants would roar twenty-four hours a day, burning coal to stoke the fires that melted the metal—businessmen would take a second shirt to the office with them every day, because by lunchtime the sweat on their necks and the smoke in the air would combine to turn their once-white collars a dark, dingy gray.

Wildlife was suffering too—and not just in the waterways. Clear-cutting forests was destroying habitats, pollutants in the air were killing insects and birds. Farmers freely sprayed pesticides to control insects that attacked crops, but the chemicals poisoned more than just the bugs. In 1962, conservationist Rachel Carson published a landmark book called *Silent Spring*, documenting, among other things, the fact that the pesticide DDT was driving the bald eagle—America's national symbol—to the edge of extinction. Rising concentrations of the pesticide were causing female eagles to lay eggs with shells that were too thin, meaning that they would break long before the chicks were ready to hatch. The current generation of bald eagles could well be the last.

By the time June 1969 arrived and the Cuyahoga burned, Americans were at a breaking point—and at least one person recognized that fact. He was Gaylord Nelson, a senator from Wisconsin, who had previously served as the state's governor, and proudly called himself the "conservation governor." During his time in office, he had battled industry to acquire more than $50 million worth of state land and set it aside not for development but for parks and wilderness that would forever remain unspoiled. When he reached the Senate in 1963, he persuaded then-president John F. Kennedy to deliver a series of speeches around the country on environmental reforms, and Kennedy—who was famous for his glamour and charisma and ability to persuade people—could not help being moved by the plain-looking man from the Midwest, who was much less glamorous, much less charismatic, but irresistibly persuasive in his own earnest way.

Not long after the Santa Barbara oil blowout, Nelson happened to be flying over the affected coastline, saw for himself the vast, sprawling slick and was sickened by it. So he had a brilliant idea—sort of.

The civil rights movement and the anti-war movement had had a lot of success with what they called sit-ins—occupying lunch counters or libraries that banned Black people, or settling in at the offices of lawmakers who were supporting the war in Vietnam and not leaving until their ideas were heard. Nelson saw the effectiveness of those demonstrations. They were stubborn and immovable, but they were also peaceful and persuasive. Not only did they often wear down the lawmakers or the people who owned the lunch counters, they also attracted media attention, which could only spread their message further. The environment was becoming a growing issue on college campuses, and since it was one requiring at least a bit of an understanding of science, Nelson decided to try to put a spin on the sit-ins, hoping to stage a series of what he would call "teach-ins" around the country.

He recruited Pete McCloskey, a California congressman and a noted environmental advocate, to work with him, as well as Denis Hayes, a graduate student at Harvard University who was already nationally renowned for organizing protests against the Vietnam War.

One of the first things Hayes and McCloskey said to Nelson was, in so many words, "You're kidding about the teach-ins, right?"

It was absolutely true that the nation had much to learn about how to care for the planet. But it was also absolutely true that people like to be stirred more than taught, energized more than lectured to. If the likes of Dr. Martin Luther King Jr., Abraham Lincoln and Kennedy himself had proven anything, it was that the best leaders must first awaken the public, move them to feel passion about an issue like racism or war or the pollution of the planet; once people care, there is much they'll be willing to learn.

So McCloskey and Hayes and ultimately Nelson decided that instead of beginning with environmental teach-ins, they would start simpler still, declaring a sort of national holiday on which Americans would celebrate the Earth, embrace the Earth, gather in cities and communities and grade schools and colleges to demonstrate a new concern for the Earth. They quickly gathered a staff of more than eighty volunteers—big enough to coordinate a nationwide movement but small enough to be nimble and controllable and work fast. And then they recruited one more unlikely person: a man named John Koenig, who was neither an activist nor environmentalist. Instead he was an advertising executive—and one of the most celebrated minds in his industry.

It was Koenig who dreamed up the ingenious series of commercials for Timex watches, in which one of the company's famously inexpensive, famously rugged $9.95 sport watches would be subjected to some kind of abuse—attached to the blades of an outboard motor, strapped to a baseball bat while New York Yankees slugger Mickey Mantle hit pitched balls—and would nonetheless keep working. The tagline, "It takes a licking and keeps on ticking," became legendary. In an era in which size was everything in American cars, Koenig also co-created the celebrated "Think Small" ad campaign for the little, imported Volkswagen—a car so compact and cute it was nicknamed "the Beetle."

For Nelson's celebration of the environment, Koenig kept things similarly simple: the event would be straightforwardly called Earth Day. It rhymed nicely with "birthday," and more important, like "Think small," it said exactly what it needed to say—not a syllable more or less. This would be a national day devoted to the planet.

By the time the group had organized, it was too late to schedule Earth Day for 1969. It was already summer, the planning would take months, and expecting people to participate in a nationwide outdoor demonstration in the cold and damp of November and December was folly. Scheduling it for the first day of the next spring—March 21, 1970—was a natural choice, nicely suggesting the idea of rebirth that the season always captured. But March was still too cold and wet in the north and the east, and college students—who would be counted on to be among the most enthusiastic participants in the demonstrations—would be busy with classes. Better to schedule it for a month later, when the weather would be warmer and the students would be on spring break.

The date thus chosen was April 22. It was a weekday, a Wednesday, which was considered ideal. Cities would be busy and full, and while college students would be on break, most public schools would be in session. Children were the people who would inherit the planet, and getting them and their teachers involved was a good way to foster environmental awareness not just for a day, but across generations.

Even with the extra few months the committee had given itself, coordinating a national event would not be easy. There was no internet, no social media, no instant organizing and fund-raising simply by reaching out to tens of millions of computers and smartphones across the nation. Instead, the eighty people who made up the main Earth Day committee set up local groups on campuses and in communities, connecting with newspapers and TV and radio stations, as well as with ordinary citizens, in the hope that they would all spread the word. The phone calls they made were all dialed by real people calling up the offices and homes of other real people and speaking to them directly. The millions of pieces of mail sent out were physical mail—manually folded, slid into envelopes, licked and stamped and hand-carried to mailboxes.

There was pushback, of course. Not every elected official thought the environment was a priority. Some believed that protecting the planet would hurt the economy if industries had to spend the money to find better, cleaner, but more expensive ways to dispose of their waste. Politicians from states that produced oil, like Texas and Oklahoma and Alaska, or produced coal, like West Virginia and Kentucky, wanted nothing to do with demonstrators who seemed to be demonizing the resource that provided jobs to many of their voters.

Nelson had a nifty way of responding to that idea: "The economy is a wholly owned subsidiary of the environment," he would say, "not the other way around." In other words, the planet can get by perfectly well without human businesses, but human businesses can hardly function in an uninhabitable world.

Not all of the objections were economic. There were some people—admittedly just a few—who saw something sinister merely in the date the Earth Day organizers had chosen. April 22, 1970, just happened to be the hundredth birthday of Vladimir Lenin, the first leader of the communist government of the Soviet Union—and in 1970, the Soviet Union was America's mortal enemy. The Daughters of the American Revolution, a volunteer organization whose members trace their roots back to people who were involved in the original fight for American independence, happened to hold their annual convention in the week leading up to Earth Day, and a delegate from Mississippi argued that the entire event was a dark Soviet plot. "Subversive elements plan to make American children live in an environment that is good for them," she said. The idea went nowhere—not least because no one could quite figure out what in the world was problematic about children living in exactly that kind of healthy environment.

The planet had no way of knowing that an entire nation of 205 million people was waking up on April 22 planning to rise in its defense, but it nonetheless cooperated in the effort. The temperatures were generally mild and the skies generally clear in the East and West, and it was sunnier and warmer still through most of the south and plains states. The Pacific Northwest was expecting some showers, but the Pacific Northwest was *always* expecting showers, and if there were any people in the country who were able to press on despite messy conditions, it was the ones who lived there.

Many businesses had adopted the Earth Day message, and a lot of them pledged to donate money or stage events in support of it. That morning's issue of the *New York Times* included a full-page ad taken out by *Seventeen* magazine—whose audience was made up of just the kind of kids and teens the Earth Day organizers were hoping to reach. It featured a picture of a young couple walking along a beach, with text that read, "Today—Earth Day—we salute millions of earnest young people who have accepted the challenge of seeking solutions for our environmental ills. Having reached the moon in the Sixties, perhaps in the Seventies we shall rediscover the earth!" If there was something a little insincere in all the corporate enthusiasm—an attempt to cash in on a good cause and, in effect, take a free ride on the work of all those earnest people—it still showed that on the side of the environment was the right place to be.

Whatever the motivations of any one business, any one town, any one person, America indeed showed the planet the love that day. In city after city, community after community, people turned out. Events were staged on 1,500 campuses and in 10,000 schools, with speeches, marches, community cleanups and even the teach-ins Nelson had so wanted. Boston schoolchildren picked up cans and bottles in vacant lots. Sacramento students did the same and even did the heavy work of gathering abandoned tires and carting them off for proper disposal. More than 1,000 students from Cleveland State University picked up trash from around the city and loaded it into garbage trucks that had been made available for the day. In New York, students from a Brooklyn high school cleaned the beaches nearby. Students in Manhattan picked up trash in a park on the Upper East Side, next to the East River and near the mayor's mansion, which was meant to be scenic but was spoiled by rubbish. College students gathered in subway stations along the dirty, neglected Lexington Avenue Line and washed the windows of the trains when they stopped in stations.

Inevitably, with college students involved and the high-spirited energy of the 1960s uprisings in play, some of the protests became equal parts theater. Students at Florida Technological University— today known as the University of Central Florida—held a trial for a Chevrolet, found it guilty of poisoning the air and sentenced it to death—though despite their efforts to destroy it with a sledgehammer, they couldn't quite carry out the execution. Students at the University of Minnesota held a solemn ceremony in which they buried an internal combustion engine. Students in Cleveland paid tribute to Cleaveland, with one rowing to more or less the spot on the Cuyahoga where the long-ago explorer was said to have come ashore. The student then looked around, declared it too dirty a place to build a colony and rowed back off.

In Denver, where the high elevation and thin air increases the destructive impact of automobile exhaust, high school students pedaled bicycles to the state capital as a symbol of protest against cars. Nelson spoke at a Denver teach-in and deftly connected the environmental movement with the anti-war movement.

"Environment is a problem perpetuated by expenditures of tens of billions of dollars a year on the Vietnam War," he said, "instead of on our decaying, crowded, congested, polluted urban areas that are inhuman traps for millions of people."

In Washington, D.C., students marched on the Department of the Interior—which is responsible for looking after the country's wilderness and national parks—and gathered on the Mall near the Washington Monument, where the civil rights march to the Lincoln Memorial began seven years before. Hayes spoke there, also connecting the environmental movement to the Vietnam War, but doing so with the stridency and passion of an activist, compared to the more measured tones of Nelson, a politician.

"Even if that war were over tomorrow," he said, "we would still be killing this planet. We are systematically destroying our land, our streams and our seas. We foul our air, deaden our senses and pollute our bodies."

New York City, determined—as it so often is—to do things bigger, better, more ostentatiously than any other place in the nation, delivered on that effort. Mayor John Lindsay closed Fifth Avenue, which runs up and down the center of Manhattan, from 14th Street to 59th Street, giving the boulevard over to marchers and speeches. Orange and blue bunting, the city's colors, hung from lampposts, and balloons stamped with environmental slogans were distributed. That the balloons would surely enter the waste stream later that day—creating mounds of garbage that were just one more part of the environmental problem—seemed, at least at the moment, less important than conveying the environmental message.

Downtown in Union Square, near New York University, booths were set up promoting various parts of the environmental cause—ending air pollution, controlling population, building cleaner cities. At least 100,000 people moved through the square that day, many of them stopping at the booths to learn more about the various issues. Con Edison, the city power company, which had been long criticized for its poor environmental record, feared protests and even violence. While it remained open for business—a power company could hardly shut down—it kept its doors locked and stationed security guards at each one. But there was no violence; these were not the angry protests in Chicago from two years earlier, when young people rose up to stop a war they might be sent to fight. This was a happy—if deeply worried—statement of love for the planet.

The demonstrations and celebrations kept going all day, all over the country, ending well after nightfall, which arrived, as it always did, with the turning of the newly appreciated Earth bringing darkness first to the Eastern time zone, then to Central, then to Mountain and then to Pacific. The question then became, what would America do when Wednesday turned to Thursday, when April 22 turned to April 23, and the nation woke up to a world that was no less filthy than it had been the day before?

As it turned out, the nation answered that question bravely and well—at least at first. Before 1970 was out, President Nixon established the Environmental Protection Agency, and Congress passed the Clean Air

Act. In 1972, the Clean Water Act followed. Cities and states established corresponding agencies and passed corresponding laws, and the worst messes of the 1970s were slowly addressed. Strict rules went into effect preventing river dumping and limiting the pollutants factories could emit from smokestacks. People learned about recycling, about separating paper from plastic from glass. Cars got smaller, which meant they got cleaner; lead was removed from gasoline, and gasoline was even removed from cars, as electric or at least hybrid models were slowly developed. The laws were unevenly enforced, and the industries tried to skirt them, but the free-for-all days of fouling the land and water and air with no limitations were over.

Environmental awareness in the United States helped foster environmental awareness throughout the world. In 1987, forty-six nations signed the Montreal Protocol, banning chlorofluorocarbons, a type of gas used in aerosol cans that was destroying the atmosphere's protective layer of ozone, allowing dangerous ultraviolet radiation to reach the surface of the planet. Ultimately, a total of 197 nations signed the agreement and the chlorofluorocarbon problem was largely eliminated.

In 1990, the United States strictly limited the emissions of sulfur dioxide from smokestacks, a pollutant that had been contributing to "acid rain," which damaged rivers, fish and wildlife, and ate away at marble and masonry. In 1997, member states of the United Nations agreed to the Kyoto Protocol, pledging to meet certain environmental cleanup targets by certain dates. In 2015, a similar but more ambitious agreement known as the Paris Agreement was signed by 195 countries.

The Great Lakes got cleaner and cleaner—if still nowhere near spotlessly so. Rivers did too, including the Cuyahoga, which, fifty years on, is still healing from the horrors of its past, but is now an American Heritage river, giving it all manner of environmental protections. It no longer burns—it hasn't since that final time in 1969—and it runs clear along much of its length. Multiple species of fish, including some finicky ones that can survive in only the cleanest water, have returned. Earth Day celebrations have been held every year since 1970, on April 22, and environmentalists pledge to honor the date forever. In 1995, then-president Bill Clinton awarded an aging Gaylord Nelson the Presidential Medal of Honor for his lifetime of environmental service.

Still, humans are a fallible species, and often a very shortsighted one. Even as we address so many of our environmental problems, we continue to create others. The oceans are increasingly contaminated by plastics, with a garbage patch measuring an astonishing 600,000 square miles—twice the size of Texas—adrift in the Pacific Ocean. Much more worrisome is the problem of climate change. Greenhouse gasses—mostly carbon dioxide—have been pouring into the atmosphere since the industrial revolution in the eighteenth century, and are raising atmospheric and ocean temperatures, leading to droughts, wildfires, floods, tornados, glacial melt, rising sea levels and violent weather events worldwide.

There are people who say climate change is a hoax. They're wrong. There are people who say it's exaggerated. They're wrong too. There are people who understand the truth—that it's a deadly serious business—but they have grown so despairing that they have come to conclude that nothing can be done. Happily, they are wrong as well. Reversing climate change will not remotely be easy, and it will not remotely be quick. It will take the lifetimes of many generations. But there's one other, more-powerful quality of the human species: we care deeply about our children and grandchildren and all the other children who will follow them. It is up to each generation to do its best to leave a cleaner and cleaner planet for the next.

Beneath a mammoth mushroom cloud, the city of Nagasaki lay in ruins after it was struck by an atom bomb on August 8, 1945.

NINE

The March Against Nuclear Weapons
1982

IT'S HARD TO know exactly how a major American city would fare in the wake of a nuclear attack—but the results wouldn't be pretty. The details would depend on just which city was hit.

Washington, D.C., would be an obvious choice for any attacker. For one thing, it's small—a tiny jigsaw piece carved out of southwestern Maryland. So compact a city could be more or less wiped out with a single bomb—provided it was the right bomb. More important, Washington is the capital of the nation, where its leaders live and work. Pick a time when the president, the vice president, the Congress and the justices of the Supreme Court would all be in town—say, on the day the president is scheduled to deliver the annual State of the Union speech—and all three branches of the United States government would vanish at once.

(The only important government official not to perish would be the one who actually goes by the informal name "the designated survivor." Whenever the president addresses Congress, with all the senators and representatives present in the Capitol building, as well as members of the Supreme Court and many members of the president's cabinet— including such powerful people as the secretary of state and secretary of defense—one Cabinet member stays away, in an undisclosed location. That way, if a disaster struck the Capitol building and everyone died, there would be one person to carry on as the acting president. Often the designated survivor is a comparatively low-ranking member of the Cabinet, such as the secretary of agriculture or transportation. In an eye blink, then, one of the least powerful people in government would be transformed into the most powerful.)

Of course, for the attacking nation there would be downsides to the idea of attacking Washington. With little of the American government left, most of the remaining power would be held by the leaders of the military, who would be in possession of America's own nuclear weapons and would surely be itching to hit back fast and hard, rather than negotiating some kind of peace. A single strike launched at the United States would likely elicit an angry storm of strikes in return.

Los Angeles, Chicago, Dallas and Atlanta—big, sprawling cities with big, sprawling economies—would likely catch the bad guys' eyes too. But the American city that is surely the biggest, most tempting target for any enemy nation is New York, especially its main borough of Manhattan. It's physically small like Washington—just 13.4 miles long and 2.3 miles wide—but it's densely populated, with nearly 1.7 million people packed onto that one scrap of land. New York City as a whole—including all five of its boroughs—is home to more than 8.6 million people. The city is also the center of American commerce and media. A strike there could throw the nation into chaos.

The world has gotten only two looks at what happens when a city comes under nuclear attack—both at the end of World War II, in 1945, when the U.S. dropped the first nuclear weapons on the Japanese cities of Hiroshima and Nagasaki, killing more than 226,000 people. At that time, those bombs were far and away the most powerful ones ever invented. The one that destroyed Hiroshima was a sixteen-kiloton weapon—meaning it had an explosive power equivalent to 16,000 tons of dynamite. The one dropped on Nagasaki packed twenty-one kilotons. In the decades since, bombs have gotten much, much bigger, now measuring their power in megatons—or a million tons of dynamite. The biggest ever built is Russia's fifty-megaton Tsar Bomba.

To help understand the possible effects of a nuclear attack, American analysts have conducted studies—originally on paper and later in computer simulations—of what would happen if a bomb of a particular size struck a particular city. One of the most thorough of the simulations involves a comparatively small 150-kiloton weapon— equivalent to 150,000 tons of dynamite—striking New York.

On the average day, there are about 125,000 people in every square mile of Manhattan. The simulation imagines a clear, pleasant day, which means that about 25 percent of those people would be outside. In this make-believe scenario, the bomb would explode in the sky just over 42nd Street, in the heart of Manhattan, where Times Square and the Broadway Theater District are located. It would likely not be dropped by an airplane but rather delivered by what's known as an intercontinental ballistic missile (ICBM), which, as its name suggests, is a rocket that can be launched from one continent, cross an ocean, and strike a target on another continent.

In the first millionth of a second after the bomb detonated, the temperature at the center of the blast would be well over 1 million degrees; the ground directly below would feel about 10,000 of those degrees, which means 42nd Street, Times Square and the Theater District would be the same temperature as the surface of the sun. Within the first second of detonation, a fireball close to half a mile wide would form, and that, plus an explosive increase in air pressure, would instantly demolish every building within that footprint, including such landmarks as the Empire State Building, Madison Square Garden and the main branch of the New York Public Library. About 75,000 people would just as instantly die—some vaporized completely.

Four seconds after detonation, the heat and the shock wave would have spread for a full mile, destroying most buildings within that circle and causing the few that remained standing to burst into flames. Four hospitals would be reduced to rubble, as would the celebrated Chrysler Building and Rockefeller Center. The headquarters of the United Nations—built in the wake of World War II, to help ensure global peace—would be destroyed as well. An additional 300,000 New Yorkers would die and 100,000 more would be injured.

At the six-second mark, the circular blast would have reached four miles, destroying or at least severely damaging any buildings it touched. In those buildings that remained standing, all the windows would explode inward, killing or injuring anyone in the path of the blast of glass. An estimated 190,000 people indoors would die, as would another 190,000 outside.

The destruction would continue to the ten-second point, with the fireball having grown to five miles; within that perimeter another 235,000 people would die and 525,000 more would be injured. People wearing dark-colored clothes, which absorb more heat and light, would suffer worse than people wearing light clothes, which reflects some light away. The immediate effects of the explosion would begin to dissipate about six seconds later, but not before the damage extended into New Jersey to the west, Long Island to the east and New York Harbor to the south. The Statue of Liberty would likely be blasted off its pedestal. In all, counting casualties outside the boundaries of the city, there would more than 1.6 million injuries and deaths on that first day. Many more tens of thousands would die later of burns and radiation sickness. Much of the land where New York used to stand would remain radioactive for years, rendering it uninhabitable.

And that's one bomb—one small bomb. There are many, many more than just that one in the world. Over the thirty years that followed the end of World War II, when only the U.S. had nuclear weapons, half a dozen more countries—the Soviet Union (which was made up of many republics, principally Russia, and broke apart in 1991), the United Kingdom, France, China, India and Israel—learned to build them. By 1975, those nuclear nations had together amassed more than 47,000 of the weapons. The human species, which emerged no more than 350,000 years earlier, had acquired the power to destroy the planet.

While all seven countries that were in possession of nuclear weapons were responsible for creating the danger, it was the U.S. and the Soviets who were far and away the most to blame. They were the two most powerful nations in the world—with the Russians dominating the eastern half of the planet and the Americans dominating the west—and they were forever competing with each other for more power. Of the 47,000 nuclear weapons that existed, the U.S. had about 19,000 and the Russians 27,000—more than enough for the two countries to wipe each other out. The fact that they kept building and stockpiling the weapons anyway was, many critics said, like two people standing waist-deep in a basement full of gasoline and arguing over who has more matches. Light even one and you're both going to die.

In the 1950s and 1960s, Americans lived in constant fear that that nuclear match would be struck. Across the country, families began digging underground chambers called fallout shelters in their backyards. If a nuclear war began, they could dive inside and slam the door, eating canned food and drinking bottled water, trapped in a single, small, windowless room for weeks or even months until the deadly radiation unleashed by the bombs and missiles had dissipated. In schools, children practiced air-raid drills, much like fire drills or lockdown drills, only in this case they would dive under their desks and cover their heads until an imaginary attack was over. A flimsy desk and a protective crouch would, of course, offer no real protection against a bomb with the power to destroy a city. But for parents and teachers and children, it was better to pretend that there was some way to stay safe than to admit there was none at all.

The leaders of the U.S. and the Soviet Union recognized the madness of what they were doing, and in the 1960s and 1970s did negotiate some treaties to limit certain kinds of nuclear weapons. But that did nothing to stop them from continuing to build the kinds the agreements did allow. Throughout the presidencies of John F. Kennedy, Lyndon Johnson, Richard Nixon, Gerald Ford and Jimmy Carter, the global bomb tally grew past 55,000—even as all of those presidents continued to promise that they were really, truly trying to figure out a way to stop the weapons race. Then, in 1980, Ronald Reagan was elected president of the United States.

Reagan, a former actor and governor of California, seemed like the friendliest, easiest, most affable man you could ever want to meet. He was sixty-nine years old—older than any other newly elected president—but he had a happy, crinkly smile, a folksy way of speaking and the ability to charm any audience he was addressing. Americans, it seemed, had chosen everybody's favorite grandfather to lead the nation.

But Reagan, like all people, had a darker side too, and in his case, it was mostly the Soviet Union that brought it out. Reagan didn't like the Soviets, and more important, he didn't trust the Soviets. He had spent much of his political career warning that the country was a global menace, and the only thing that could stop it from threatening every other country on the planet was a strong America with a powerful military. If it took building more warships, fighter jets and battle tanks to do that, he would do it. And if it took stacking more nuclear weapons on top of the deadly pile the country already had, he would do that too.

The bomb building that had begun in the 1940s would, it seemed, accelerate in the 1980s, with no way out of the problem. No country in the world would be the first to give up its nuclear weapons and make itself vulnerable to all the others that still had them. As long as anyone held on to the bombs, everyone would.

But what if—just as a first step to control the insanity—countries agreed to a nuclear freeze? What if they promised that they would at least build no more weapons, capping their arsenals at their current size and then slowly begin talking about how to reduce the stockpiles? Surely even the most aggressive, most suspicious country would be willing to try that.

The people of the United States could not dictate what other countries did, but they could try to influence American policies and thereby set a good example for the rest of the world. So in 1980, activists once again began to mobilize. Across the country, local groups began organizing to persuade state legislatures and the U.S. Congress to pass resolutions supporting a nuclear freeze. The proposals would have no force of law, but the more states that approved, the more powerful the message would be. By 1982, resolutions had been introduced in nine state legislatures and approved in eight. The U.S. Congress had agreed to consider the matter too.

Local action, however, would be nothing like national action. Just as civil rights demonstrators in the various states knew the kind of impact a march on Washington could have, just as anti-war protesters on college campuses knew the kind of attention a demonstration in Chicago during a national political convention would attract, so too did proponents of a nuclear freeze know they needed one great gathering in one great place to shout their message to the world.

Circumstance handed them just the right place and time. On June 7, 1982, the United Nations was going to convene a special session to discuss nuclear weapons, in which all of its 157 member countries could negotiate how to start ridding the world of the worst weapons ever invented. The conference would be held at the U.N.'s headquarters in New York City—the very city that would be so easy to kill and so hard to rebuild if a nuclear attack ever came for real. When the delegates arrived that June, the protesters would be there to greet them.

The nuclear weapon's ability to do damage at such a huge scale is the result of physics playing out at a tiny scale. It was Albert Einstein, the great physicist, who first discovered that matter—a rock, a tree, a shoe, a spoon—is more than just the minerals or metal or other stuff it's made of. It's also energy. That shouldn't make a bit of sense. How can the power that moves, say, a baseball through the air be the same thing as the ball? But in some ways it is, especially down at the level of the atom. Split the right kind of atom the right way and it will give off a powerful burst of the energy that makes it up.

The first nuclear bombs relied on that business of breaking atoms— or fission. The bomb that destroyed Hiroshima carried a two-pound sphere of a heavy, unstable element known as uranium-235. Inside the bomb, a bullet made of the same material was fired into the sphere and set off a chain reaction of fracturing atoms that caused a blast vastly more powerful than two pounds of an ordinary explosive like dynamite or gunpowder ever could.

When the bomb was first tested in the empty deserts of Los Alamos, New Mexico, J. Robert Oppenheimer, the scientist who led the U.S. nuclear weapons program, watched the blast in both wonder and horror. He thought of a line from Hindu scripture: "Now I am become Death, destroyer of worlds."

Even more powerful than a bomb that split atoms would be a bomb that did the opposite—squeezed them together so powerfully they combined. That process, known as fusion, is what powers the sun itself, with hydrogen atoms fusing into helium atoms and, in the process, releasing enough energy to light the entire solar system. The fusion bombs were the ones that took the destructive power of nuclear weapons from the kiloton level to the megaton, making it possible to destroy not just individual cities but virtually all life on Earth. Those were also the ones that made a nuclear freeze so important.

It was Randall Forsberg, an expert in international relations, who first suggested that a freeze might be a big step toward climbing down from the nuclear cliff. When people read the papers written by Randall Forsberg and then actually *met* Randall Forsberg they were often confused, because the writer's full name was Randall Caroline Forsberg and she was a woman—one whose parents simply liked the name Randall. When Forsberg began her career, in 1968, she did so in the only way many women could at the time, which was as a typist, in her case at the Stockholm International Peace Research Institute, a group that helped countries find ways to resolve conflicts without going to war.

Work like that was a natural fit for Forsberg. She was born in Huntsville, Alabama, where both the rockets for America's space program and the missiles that carried nuclear weapons were built. The grandeur of a machine intended for space and the horror of a machine intended for war were impossible to separate; the difference was all in the choices human beings made about how to use their inventions. Forsberg became consumed by the peacemaking work she did in Stockholm and in 1974 moved back to the United States to get her doctoral degree in international studies at the Massachusetts Institute of Technology. By 1979, she was *Dr.* Randall Forsberg, and in her new capacity, she established the Institute for Defense and Disarmament Studies, in Cambridge, Massachusetts, to promote the idea of a nuclear freeze.

Forsberg's writings and speeches were what inspired the freeze resolutions that were being proposed in the state legislatures and in Congress. It was those writings too that, in January 1982, motivated a group of activists in New York City to reach out to dozens of other groups around the country with the idea that they should all pull together to stage a collective freeze march in New York City. The date they chose was June 12, the first Saturday after the U.N. disarmament meetings began. Then, too busy to come up with a name for their group, they simply called themselves the June 12 Rally Committee and got straight to work.

A June 12 march meant that the group had just six months to do their work. Borrowing from the organizational structure used by the March on Washington planners, the New York committee coordinated with the state committees, which coordinated with the local committees, which coordinated with the neighborhood and community and college committees. The Southern Christian Leadership Conference—established during the Montgomery bus boycott of 1955—helped lead the effort; so too did the American Friends Service Committee, a peace organization established by the Quaker religion—the same religion that played such an important role in the 1848 Seneca Falls Convention for women's rights. As with the March on Washington, entertainers would again be booked, but these were entertainers of a generation later: James Taylor, Bruce Springsteen, Linda Ronstadt, Joan Baez, Jackson Browne—people who had grown up in the era of the fallout shelters and the air raid drills, all of whom were now hugely popular and hugely famous and figured they might be able to use some of their influence to help spare the next generations of children the terrors they had experienced.

The rally to keep the world safe from nuclear extinction began at New York's Dag Hammarskjöld Plaza, which was in some ways a terrible idea because it was not remotely designed to hold half a million people, and that's what it seemed the crowd would number that day. Built to honor the second secretary general of the United Nations—the U.N.'s highest position—the plaza is an open, public space between 46th and 47th Streets at the foot of a forty-nine-story office building, close to U.N. headquarters. On a pleasant day, it's a nice place to push a baby carriage, take in the sun or sit on a bench and read.

On the morning of June 12—a cool, cloudy day, when there was little sun to be had—hundreds of thousands of people began converging on the plaza, quickly filled it and then spilled out north and south along Manhattan's nearby avenues, as well as east toward the U.N. complex itself. It was the very fact that the U.N. was so nearby—near enough that it would be impossible for the delegates and ambassadors there not to see what was happening outside their windows—that convinced the rally committee to choose the plaza as the place to start the day's activities. From there, the crowd would begin the three-mile march to a much larger site: the fifty-five-acre Great Lawn in Central Park, which very much was designed with a crush of hundreds of thousands of people in mind. Just the year before, a crowd of 400,000 had gathered there to see a performance by the folk-rock duo Simon & Garfunkel. It was a record for the Great Lawn, but it was a record that would be broken that day.

Before the march began that morning, there would be a few

speeches at the Plaza site, but *only* a few. Half a million people was too big a crowd to expect to stand and listen for long. Politicians were not invited to speak—at least not politicians who were at that point running for some office. Nobody wanted a candidate exploiting the universal message of peace to try to win votes. That rule excluded the mayor of New York, Ed Koch, a big, loud man with a big, loud personality who liked nothing more than to address a crowd, but who was also running for governor in that fall's election and was thus disqualified from speaking.

"While I suppose most rallies would like to have the mayor welcome them," he groused to a reporter from the *New York Times* who was on the scene, "that's all right with me and I said I understand it." People who knew Koch suspected he actually did not understand it one tiny bit.

The half million people were instead welcomed by Carol Bellamy, the president of the New York City Council, who was not currently up for reelection. Bellamy had familiarized herself with the power of nuclear weapons, and what she had learned seemed to have unsettled her.

"Look around you for just one moment, my friends, at the beauty of New York's urban landscape," she said. "Then consider that the detonation of a single one-megaton bomb would flatten every building in sight. The flash of white light, the force of the fireball, would within seconds char, batter and crush every living being within a nine-mile radius, the winds spreading radiation and fire far beyond."

It was a terrible image, but an honest image. If it was a dark way to begin so big a day, there was hope in the air all the same.

"There's no way the leaders can ignore this now," said one member of the crowd, who had driven 240 miles from Utica, New York, to be there that day.

Another marcher, who had traveled a decidedly greater 10,000 miles, from Melbourne, Australia—a flight that can take more than twenty-one hours—glanced toward the U.N. complex.

"This should guarantee that those blokes in the big house will do the right thing," he said.

Whether they would or would not do the right thing, the march proceeded—and even with the menace Bellamy had invoked hanging over the proceedings, there was no denying that it was an exercise in joy. The crowd flowed west and then split into two great rivers of people, both moving north—one along Fifth Avenue, the other along Seventh Avenue. They would enter Central Park from its southern end and from its eastern side, and they would do so happily—dancing, singing, holding hands, chanting.

Five thousand police officers had been deployed for the event, but unlike Chicago in 1968, where the police came spoiling for a fight and the demonstrators came prepared to give them one, both groups today seemed part of the same peaceful purpose. Paper folded into the shape of a crane—the elegant water bird found around the world—is a symbol of healing in Japan, and it was adopted as a symbol of peace by the June 12 rally. Near 42nd Street, three police officers wore paper crane necklaces someone in the crowd had given them.

"Out of uniform?" a young man joked as he walked by them.

"No, no, this is the uniform for today," responded one of the officers.

The chants too reflected a peaceful agreement on the purpose of the day. During the Vietnam protests of the 1960s, demonstrators would chant, "One, two, three, four, we don't want your f—ing war," practically spitting the angry f-word. Today the chant was less aggressive, more earnest: "One, two, three, four, we don't want a nuclear war. Five, six, seven, eight, we don't want to radiate!"

Jugglers performed as they marched to the park. Parade floats mixed with the marchers. Kazoos tooted and drums banged and a golden retriever trotted along, wearing a sign that read DOGS FOR DISARMAMENT. The march flowed past St. Patrick's Cathedral on Fifth Avenue, where a couple had just gotten married. They came outside, briefly joined the crowd and kissed for the cameras that flashed all around them. Children were present everywhere as well—the young generation that might not get to grow into an older generation if the blokes in the big house, as well as the ones in Washington and Moscow and every other capital of every other country that possessed nuclear weapons, did not listen to what the people were telling them.

"We all want to be here in ten years," said one twelve-year-old boy who had flown from Evanston, Illinois, with his father.

A nine-year-old boy marched along with his mother and sister and saw danger not only to his own life, but to the America still to come. "If there is a nuclear war, a lot of us children will die," he said, "and some of us could be very important to the future of America."

A much older woman on Fifth Avenue, whose own future was mostly past, watched the marchers go by. "I've got eight grandchildren and two great-grandchildren," she told a reporter. "Those are my reasons for being out here today."

All the way at the other end of the arc of life, a baby in the parade was being carried in its mother's arms. The baby needed to eat, and the mother stopped and knelt and began to breastfeed. Applause and smiles broke out all around. "That's what this is all about," said one of the marchers.

The day proceeded peacefully, almost perfectly—but sometimes chillingly too. A group of marchers dressed in white danced and twirled and carried poles with huge white doves made of cloth and paper. A sign identified them as the world before a war. They were followed by other people in purposely stark, dark, gruesome costumes—skeletons, monsters, demons, splashed with paint meant to look like blood. It was the world after a war.

Once the crowd was inside the park, they listened to a speech by Coretta Scott King, the activist and widow of Martin Luther King Jr., who had been murdered while campaigning for justice and peace fourteen springs earlier. "We have come here in numbers so large that the message must get through to the White House and Capitol Hill," she said.

Springsteen and Baez and the other stars performed their songs— giving away music that people would usually have to buy tickets to hear. Picnic baskets were opened, bottles of wine were poured, babies played on blankets, toddlers ran through the grass. There were no arrests; there were no fights. There was only a celebration of life—and an unmistakable plea that it be allowed to endure.

The coverage of the rally in the next day's newspapers was like that for no other demonstration before. The *Washington Post* marveled that the march took on "the gaiety of a crafts fair." The *New York Times* described the diversity of the crowd as "a spectrum of humanity." The reporters struggled to reach a consensus on just how many people had participated. The half a million estimate was the one cited most, but some put it closer to 550,000 or 650,000. Some even suggested it might have crossed one million. The *Times*'s Anna Quindlen, who was just twenty-nine, might have captured it best: "A crowd the size of a fair-sized city" was how she described the masses who had descended on her town.

No matter the size of the gathering, Quindlen understood its power: "Any public demonstration is a leap of faith," she wrote, "evidence of an optimistic belief . . . that a single human being, if there are enough of them, can make a difference."

If that were so, though, the difference would be a while in coming. The gathering in New York did not lead to a nuclear freeze. Instead, the next year the global nuclear weapons count rose to 59,350; the following year it crossed 60,000, on its way to a historic peak of 64,449 in 1986. Less than nine months after the march, President Reagan delivered a speech in which he described the Soviet Union as an "evil empire," making it clear that he was in no mood to trust his mortal enemy.

The next year, while checking his microphone before delivering a radio address, he began to speak as if he were actually on the air and said, "My fellow Americans, I'm pleased to tell you today that I have signed legislation that will outlaw Russia forever. We begin bombing in five minutes."

He meant it as a joke—although a dark one—and the people around him laughed. His words were not broadcast, but they were captured on tape by radio stations that were preparing to carry his speech, and the recording quickly leaked to the public. Leaders of the Soviet Union heard the tape and seethed; the Russian news service declared the remark "unprecedentedly hostile." It was a sobering reminder of how easy it would be for a joke about bombing to turn into actual bombing.

But Reagan was a father, he was a grandfather, and if he disliked the Soviets, he loved his country, and—as his otherwise sunny disposition so often suggested—humanity itself. Like most world leaders, he knew he had a responsibility to the planet and that controlling nuclear arms was part of that. He knew it, in part, because so many Americans showed that they cared deeply about the issue on that beautiful day in New York City. What he needed was a partner with whom he could work, and in 1985, he got one, when a Russian official named Mikhail Gorbachev became the leader of the Soviet Union. Gorbachev was very different from the country's previous leaders, who had denied the Russian people freedom of speech, the right to assemble and even the right to leave the country at all. He wanted a different kind of nation and called for *glasnost*, or openness, and *perestroika*, or restructuring and reform.

In 1986, he and Reagan met in Reykjavík, Iceland, to discuss a treaty to reduce the number of nuclear weapons. Before long, they began contemplating something far more dramatic: actually eliminating the weapons, reducing the arsenals to zero by the year 2000. But that was too big a reach for two enemy nations, and after just two days, the talks collapsed. Still, both sides got a glimpse of a nuclear-free world, and they liked what they saw. The next year, they did sign a nuclear treaty, this one to limit the production of nuclear missiles that could fly short and medium distances. It didn't limit the intercontinental kind, but it was a start. The next year, they signed another deal that would oblige the two countries to notify each other at least twenty-four hours before they launched any test missiles, to prevent the experiment from being mistaken for an attack and triggering a nuclear war by accident.

Over the twenty-two years that followed, under Presidents George H. W. Bush, Bill Clinton, George W. Bush and Barack Obama, seven more nuclear treaties would be signed, and the global stockpiles of nuclear weapons would slowly fall from their record high of nearly 65,000 to just 14,575, or less than 23 percent of the amount that existed in 1986. But the news was hardly all good. In 1998, Pakistan acquired nuclear weapons—matching the power of its cross-border enemy, India, and creating just the kind of deadly standoff that existed for so long between the U.S. and the Soviet Union. In 2006, North Korea, which has been ruled for decades by a series of secretive and unpredictable leaders, became a nuclear nation too. In 2019, President Donald

Trump suspended the 1987 treaty Reagan signed with Gorbachev, claiming Russia had been cheating on the terms, and increasing tensions between the two countries.

And, of course, a global count of 14,575 nuclear weapons, while much lower than it used to be, is still 14,575 more than it should be. It takes just one bomb to unleash suffering and death. It takes just a few to wipe out an entire nation. It is the leaders of past generations who created the devices that still menace the world. Fairly or not, it will be up to the leaders of the coming generations, who are not responsible for the problem, to solve it.

Larry Kramer, photographed in 2007, at Washington Square Park in New York City.

TEN

ACT UP
1987

AN ODD LITTLE item appeared in the news on June 5, 1981. Most people weren't likely to see it, and it would have been hard for them to find it even if they'd been looking for it. The little item was not carried in the major newspapers or on network TV. It appeared instead in a newsletter released by the U.S. Centers for Disease Control (CDC), called the *Morbidity and Mortality Weekly Report.* Anything with the words "morbidity" and "mortality" in its name was not likely to be much fun, but for doctors and especially for epidemiologists—the people who study the way diseases appear and spread—it was important weekly reading.

The June 5 item reported on a tiny outbreak of a fairly common disease: five cases of pneumonia that had turned up at three different hospitals in Los Angeles, California. Pneumonia might have killed a lot of people in centuries past and it could still be deadly, but mostly for people who were very old, very young or very frail. And five cases in a city of three million people was hardly a cause for much worry.

But these five cases were different—and troubling. For one thing, the particular type of pneumonia—known as *Pneumocystis carinii pneumonia* (PCP)—was extremely rare. It occurred exclusively in people who had problems with their immune systems—the body's army of disease-fighting cells that battle bacteria and viruses and other tiny invaders. In healthy people, PCP wouldn't have a chance. The second the fungus that caused the disease attacked the body, the immune system would rise up and clobber it.

What's more, the five people who had contracted PCP were not very old, very young or very frail. They were five young men, all in their twenties or thirties—the age at which the body should be at its best, toughest and strongest. And there was the additional fact that all five of them were gay. That, certainly, should not have made any difference. Some diseases may attack one age group more than another, or even one gender more than another. But one sexual orientation more than another? That simply didn't happen.

It was a puzzle, but it was one that would have to be solved: two of the five young men had already died, and there seemed to be little hope for the other three.

Then, less than a month later, things got much worse—and much scarier. On July 3—the Friday that kicked off the Fourth of July weekend—another news report appeared, and this time it wasn't in some obscure medical publication. This time it was the *New York Times*. The paper reported on an outbreak of a type of skin cancer known as Kaposi's sarcoma (KS) in forty-one people in New York and Los Angeles. Once again, the victims were young gay men. And once again the particular disease made no sense. KS was rare—about two cases out of every three million people on the planet. And it typically affected old men in the Mediterranean region—not young men in Los Angeles and New York.

It was easy and it was tempting to conclude that the KS and PCP cases were connected—but easy and tempting conclusions are not the kind that science likes to reach. Science demands evidence and facts and experimental proof. For now, there were just clues—but they pointed to something ominous. The immune systems of all of the men in both groups were collapsing. When doctors studied their blood, they found that the disease-fighting cells known as T cells were in particular trouble, dying off and leaving the body unable to resist even a minor infection. It wasn't clear what was causing the problem, but a person without a functioning immune system was a person who was certain to die.

No one could know it at the time, but on that sunny, July 4 weekend, a terrible storm had begun to gather. More cases of collapsed immune systems and rare infections began turning up in more gay men, not just in New York and Los Angeles, but in San Francisco and Miami and Chicago and Washington, D.C., and in all of the cities where vibrant gay communities had been rising and flourishing since the great Stonewall uprising of a dozen years before.

By the end of the year, 270 cases of the mystery disease had been diagnosed in gay men, and 121 of them had died. Since the doctors had no clear idea what was causing the disease, they gave it a name that simply described what it was: gay-related immune deficiency (GRID). That seemed fitting, except it soon turned out that while gay men were the overwhelming majority of the victims, the disease was also claiming people who weren't gay, but who had hemophilia—a disease that prevents blood from clotting and that requires patients to receive frequent blood transfusions. It was also striking people who used dirty needles to inject dangerous drugs like heroin. Some women began getting sick too, and eventually their babies contracted the disease as well.

So the illness was renamed AIDS, for acquired immune deficiency syndrome—the "acquired" part meaning that you weren't born with it, but picked it up somehow; and the "syndrome" part meaning it wasn't just a single illness like a cold, but rather a whole series of illnesses that would attack people without the protection of a functioning immune system.

Whatever the disease was called, it kept killing—and killing and killing. By 1982, there had been 771 cases and 618 deaths in the U.S., and scientists had come to conclude it was probably caused by a mysterious virus—the likes of which no one had seen before. Gay men were passing it to one another through sexual encounters; women were contracting it through sexual encounters with infected husbands and partners, and were passing it to babies while they were still in the womb or later, through breast feeding; intravenous drug users were passing it to one another if they shared dirty needles; and the nation's very blood supply seemed to have became contaminated when people who did not know they were infected donated blood.

The disease roared into 1983, with the case count climbing to 2,807 and the death toll to 2,118; it got worse still in 1984, with 7,239 cases and 5,596 deaths. That year, the virus responsible—named the human immunodeficiency virus (HIV)—was at last isolated, which allowed doctors to begin trying to develop a vaccine and to spot the infection in the blood before people got sick. But identifying the virus did little to slow the infectious wildfire. Before long, tens of thousands of Americans were sick, and then more than 100,000, with young gay men still hit the hardest. AIDS burned through whole neighborhoods in major cities, leaving communities gutted, hospitals full. Parents who may have just learned to embrace and celebrate their gay sons now buried them. Gay men who had at last felt free to find love now buried their partners.

The nation was terrified—as it should have been—and millions of people felt deep concern and compassion for the suffering being visited on so many. But millions more did not—and that said something unsettling.

Americans sees themselves as a compassionate people—perhaps never more so than when they're rising up to battle a disease. In the 1940s and 1950s, the medical community and the government mobilized themselves to eradicate polio—a disease that paralyzed children—and by 1955, the first vaccine had been developed. In 1971, President Richard Nixon declared a national war on cancer and again people joined hands to fight that disease too.

But AIDS? No. People feared the disease—and feared the people who were infected with it. Gay men in hospitals waiting for their meals would find that nurses had left their tray on the floor outside their door, rather than going in and handing it to them—even though it was impossible to contract the disease simply by being around someone who had it. Men who were sick were fired from their jobs, denied apartments they tried to rent or homes they tried to buy. Ryan White, a thirteen-year-old hemophiliac who lived in Kokomo, Indiana, and contracted AIDS through a blood transfusion in 1984, was denied the right to return to school and mingle with classmates who feared being near him. President Ronald Reagan, who assumed office in 1981, did not mention AIDS publicly for the first time until 1985, by which point nearly 13,000 Americans had been killed by the disease.

Worse, the nation's drug companies did not seem to care. Research on drugs to prevent or treat AIDS was advancing at a creep, moving along at a pace that would take many years before even a single new medication would be available—despite the fact that people were getting sick and dying now, today. Worse, the drugs that did exist were far too expensive. A single year's supply of a drug called AZT, which could help slow the replication of HIV in the body, cost $10,000—and the companies showed no willingness to lower the price in the face of a national medical emergency.

Everywhere people with AIDS looked, backs were being turned on them. Health insurance would not cover their treatments; cities would not provide beds for homeless people suffering from the disease; politicians may have been sympathetic to hemophiliacs and babies with the disease, but gay men were a different matter: this was the price of homosexuality, they said—the dying young men had brought this on themselves.

Finally, the gay community had enough. Finally, like so many oppressed groups throughout history—like other gay men in 1969 who were fed up with being harassed at bars like the Stonewall—they decided to take action. The moment came on the evening of March 10, 1987, at the Gay and Lesbian Community Center on 13th Street in Manhattan, where Larry Kramer was scheduled to give a talk.

Kramer was gay, so-far uninfected and a celebrated screenwriter, author and playwright—best known for his AIDS-themed play *The Normal Heart*, which opened in 1985. Four years before that, in 1982, he had cofounded the Gay Men's Health Crisis (GMHC), a group that helped AIDS patients find care and housing. The GMHC was a hardworking group—and a well-mannered and law-abiding group too. But like every other group working to battle AIDS, it found itself slowed by the indifference of government and the pharmaceutical industry. So maybe, Kramer thought, being well-mannered and law-abiding would no longer be enough. Maybe it was time to make noise—even to break laws if that's what it took.

Kramer took the stage in the community center's auditorium as scheduled that evening. The lights were down in the audience as they would be during any talk or performance, but he didn't want that.

"Turn the house lights up, please," he said to the stage manager. The lights rose and the people in the audience looked at one another, blinking in the sudden brightness. Kramer gazed out across the hall. "I'd like two-thirds of you to stand up," he said. The audience, made up mostly of gay men, obliged, with more or less two out of every three of them rising. And then Kramer spoke a hard truth: "You could all be dead in five years at the rate we're going," he said.

His numbers were correct. The plague was moving that fast, the death rate was climbing that dizzyingly. He asked the audience to sit back down and then got straight to his point.

"If my speech tonight doesn't scare the sh—t out of you, we're in trouble," he said. "I sometimes think we have a death wish. I think we must want to die. I have never been able to understand why we have sat back and let ourselves literally be knocked off man by man, without fighting back. I have heard of denial, but this is more than denial—it is a death wish. It's your fault, boys and girls. It's our fault."

They were angry words, outrageous words—blaming the victims for the epidemic that was killing them. But they were intended to out-rage. Kramer wanted his audience good and angry, because angry people are motivated people. He spent the rest of his talk outlining a plan of action for seizing control of the epidemic and, for the gay com-munity in New York and everywhere, seizing control of their own lives. He would form a new group, more aggressive than the GMHC, called the AIDS Coalition to Unleash Power. The group would be better known by its initials: ACT UP—and in the months and years to follow, its members would do just that.

Every good political movement is at least partly a publicity movement. Activists have an idea to get across and ideals to promote and they have to do it in a memorable way. Throwing tea in Boston Harbor in 1773 was not enough all by itself to make a great nation like Great Britain offer independence to its colonies, but it made clear in an unmistakable way that those colonies were willing to seize that freedom on their own. Dr.

Martin Luther King Jr.'s four-word declaration "I have a dream" was nothing *but* words—but they were words that moved an entire nation toward justice. ACT UP would need its own powerful symbols and its own powerful words—and its members had the talent to produce them.

The advertising industry was one of the few professions in America that welcomed gay men and women in the 1980s, which meant that ACT UP had a natural pool of volunteers who knew how to make an impression. If you could create an advertising campaign that would make people want to buy a particular line of clothing or a particular soft drink, surely you could create one that would make the public understand why it was important to save lives that were being lost to a disease. Straightaway, the ACT UP artists had an idea.

During World War II, the millions of people the Nazis imprisoned in concentration camps around Europe were required to wear various insignia sewn to their prison uniforms that identified their background. Jews were made to wear yellow stars, and the rest of the groups in the camps wore triangles of different colors—red for political prisoners, black for the Roma people and some others, purple for the Jehovah's Witnesses, green for people the Germans considered criminals. For gay people, the triangle was pink.

Over the decades that followed, the pink triangle had become a sign of shame for the gay and lesbian community, and the people of ACT UP decided they were done running from it. They could never undo history, but they could snatch back the pink triangle and make it a symbol not of victimhood but of pride. On the concentration camp uniforms, the triangle pointed down, so the first thing the ACT UP graphic designers who were creating posters and flyers would do was reverse it, making it point proudly up. But there was more too.

Across generations, gay men and women had learned that it was unsafe to talk about who they were and whom they loved. That was bad enough before AIDS emerged, but such secrecy could now be deadly, because if you had to keep your sexual orientation to yourself, how could you talk to a doctor and to the rest of the gay and lesbian community and learn how to stay healthy? So underneath the proud pink triangle would be the simple motto: SILENCE = DEATH.

It was stark—and it was meant to be stark; it was chilling—and it was meant to be that too. Lives were at stake and the clock was ticking. More people were getting sick every day, and for those already sick, the urgent need for new drugs to halt the spread of the disease meant that every second counted. For that reason, ACT UP introduced a second, simple slogan: "Drugs into Bodies." That's what they were asking for: effective, affordable medications that could be developed fast, approved fast and raced to market so they could begin to treat the sick.

For Kramer and the other leaders of ACT UP, the first and best place to make that point was on Wall Street in New York City, where the New York Stock Exchange is located. There were two very big challenges to getting drugs into bodies: First, it was important to force the Food and Drug Administration (FDA)—the government body that tests and approves drugs—to speed up its processes. It could take up to nine years for a new drug to move through the testing process before it reached the market—which was far more time than most AIDS patients had to live in the first place. Once drugs were approved, the cost kept them completely out of reach of all but the wealthiest patients. It was the drug companies that set those prices—and it was at the stock exchange on Wall Street where most major American companies sold shares of themselves to investors, allowing everyday people to buy and own small pieces of the company. The more shares a company sold, the richer it would become. If no one bought the shares—or people sold the ones they already owned—the companies would lose money.

On March 24, 1987, ACT UP decided to storm Wall Street to

shame the drug companies into working with the FDA to develop and release drugs faster and sell them for lower prices. That morning, a crowd of 250 demonstrators showed up outside of the stock exchange, chanting, carrying signs, preventing traffic from moving and distributing a list of demands, including the immediate release of seven new experimental drugs and a cut in the $10,000 price of AZT.

The protesters took direct aim at the drug company Burroughs Wellcome, which manufactured AZT, carrying signs that demanded investors sell their shares. Seventeen protesters were arrested—which was exactly what they wanted. Scenes of police officers detaining people who were fighting for their lives made for powerful images on the evening news, just like the scenes of the protesters who had been arrested in Birmingham, Alabama, during the campaign for civil rights there in 1963.

The ACT UP protesters returned to Wall Street for two more demonstrations after that, and each time made sure their protests were louder and bigger. The second time more than a hundred people were arrested. The third time, the demonstrators did not confine their protest to the streets outside the exchange. Instead, seven of them slipped into the stock exchange itself, sneaked up to the balcony overlooking the vast floor where shares were bought and sold and chained themselves to the railing so that the police could not remove them easily. They then scattered counterfeit hundred-dollar bills down to the trading floor to protest the price of the AIDS drugs, and they unfurled a banner that read SELL WELLCOME. That image spread everywhere, and Burroughs Wellcome finally gave in. Several days later, the company slashed the price of AZT from $10,000 for a year's dose to $6,400. It was still expensive—too expensive for many people—but it showed that the ACT UP protesters could make a difference.

Even then, however, the AIDS plague marched pitilessly on. In

1988, more than 4,500 people died of the disease in the United States. By 1989, the number leapt beyond 14,500; in 1990 another 18,500 died. But as the disease marched on so did the protesters.

On October 11, 1988, they took aim at the FDA itself, descending on the agency's headquarters in a Washington suburb and effectively shutting it down. People who came to work could not get inside. People who had already arrived could not work for the noise in the streets. The protesters carried signs that, as always, were meant to shock: WE DIE, THEY DO NOTHING! one of them read. Another featured what looked like a bloody handprint with the words THE GOVERNMENT HAS BLOOD ON ITS HANDS: ONE AIDS DEATH EVERY HALF HOUR. Still another featured images of skulls, with the words TIME ISN'T THE ONLY THING THE FDA IS KILLING.

The chants were meant to be ugly too: "Hey, hey, FDA, how many people have you killed today?" the demonstrators called, echoing an earlier Vietnam War–era chant.

The protesters targeted local governments too. That same month, they demonstrated outside a glamorous new skyscraper on Fifth Avenue in Manhattan, built by the developer Donald Trump. The Trump organization had gotten a $6.2 million tax break—a cut in the taxes it owed the city—to make it easier to build the building. But that $6.2 million could have done more than simply give wealthy New Yorkers another place to buy luxury apartments. It could instead have helped provide housing and care for homeless New Yorkers with AIDS. At that moment there were 10,000 such people—and the city had just sixty-four beds for them.

Inevitably, the ACT UP demonstrators did go too far. The Catholic Church did not generally support the gay community, condemning homosexuality as immoral and objecting to safe-sex education that could help curb the spread of AIDS. It was natural that ACT UP and the church would clash; the question was how.

On Sunday, December 10, 1989, a huge crowd of 4,500 ACT UP protesters gathered outside of St. Patrick's Cathedral in New York—perhaps the Catholic Church's most recognizable symbol in America—while Sunday mass was being performed inside. A few dozen of the protesters also entered the church, chanting slogans and lying down in the aisles, entirely disrupting the service. For worshippers, it was a violation of a sacred ritual; for the protesters, it was one more action necessary to save their own lives. There the moral standoff might have remained, with both sides deeply committed to what they felt was right.

One protester, however, tipped that balance. Finding a communion wafer, he broke it up and threw it to the floor. For non-Catholics that might not mean much—a little broken cracker that could easily be swept up. But for believers, the meaning was different: for them, the communion wafer is literally the body of Jesus Christ, and to do what the protester did was a profound desecration. In that act lay the tension in all public demonstrations: What is enough to achieve your ends and what pushes so far that it hurts the larger cause?

New York City mayor David Dinkins and New York State governor Mario Cuomo condemned the demonstration. A spokesman for the Coalition for Gay and Lesbian Rights—which would normally support the ACT UP mission—called the action "stupid and wrong-headed." One member of ACT UP itself openly called the St. Patrick's demonstration an "utter failure." It was an important lesson—for ACT UP, for all organized demonstrators—in the tricky business of persuading without enraging, arguing without alienating.

Still, on the whole there were smarts behind the street theater, and that was the genius of ACT UP. The members of the group did more than just stage events; they also worked quietly and doggedly to become experts in the field of AIDS care. They knew the drugs that were being tested; they knew how the approval process worked—with experiments first in test tubes, then in animals, then in groups of actual patients—and they knew all of the ways those protocols could be simplified. They wrote to the doctors and health administrators in the government, attended meetings with them, offered their help and their insight. Eventually, the doctors began listening to them, drew them in, had them join their boards and decision-making bodies and accepted many of their ideas. Drugs did start flowing faster; in some people who had the disease, the symptoms advanced more slowly.

Not long after the St. Patrick's Cathedral demonstration, a former New York City health commissioner, who had himself been the target of ACT UP's anger, admitted the impact the group had. "There's no doubt they've had a tremendous effect," he said. "We've basically changed the way we make drugs available in the last year."

Dr. Anthony Fauci, then and now the director of the National Institute of Allergy and Infectious Diseases, was publicly dismissed by Kramer as "an incompetent idiot," but he could not help but admit the difference Kramer and his group had made. "Did ACT UP play a significant role in the whole idea of expanded access to experimental drugs?" he asked once. "The answer is yes."

In the United States, the AIDS plague at last ran into a drug it could not defeat. The virus that had eluded so many attempts to kill it or at least tame it has a weak spot, deep in the part of its molecular structure that allows it to replicate—or reproduce itself. Drugs known as antiretrovirals (ARVs), approved in 1996, could disrupt that process, crippling the virus's ability to make copies of itself. AIDS patients who had the virus in their bodies probably always would, but as long as they stayed on the drugs, the infection could be held to such low levels that some blood tests could not even detect it. People who would have been doomed to die in the days when ACT UP was forming could now live their lives fully.

Antiretroviral drugs remain expensive, and the battle goes on in the United States and elsewhere to make them available at prices people can afford. In much of the rest of the world, especially in Africa, where AIDS remains an epidemic and the drugs are not widely available, the suffering endures. In 2018, nearly 37 million people worldwide were infected with HIV and nearly 1 million people died of AIDS. But many people don't die, and many more, thanks to AIDS education programs that ACT UP helped develop, never get sick in the first place.

As of the writing of this book, Kramer is eighty-three years old. In 1988, he too was diagnosed with HIV, but he lived long enough to be able to take advantage of ARVs when they were developed. Today, he looks older than his actual age, but his temperament is much the same. He is loud, cranky, provocative, and he likes himself just fine that way. In 2017, the *New York Times* ran a profile about him and titled it "Twilight of a Difficult Man."

"I was trying to make people united and angry," he said to the *Times*. "I was known as the angriest man in the world, mainly because I discovered that anger got you further than being nice. And when we started to break through in the media, I was better TV than someone who was nice."

The hard truth of public protest is that it often takes very angry men and women, difficult men and difficult women to make the world a better, safer, more just place. They inflame us—and they save us. We are better for having them among us.

Protesters, some in "Pussyhats," demonstrate for women's rights.

ELEVEN

The Women's March
2017

THERE WAS A lot that didn't happen at the Jacob K. Javits Convention Center in New York City in the early morning hours of November 9, 2016. That came as a surprise because things were supposed to be awfully exciting at that time on that day in that part of the city. Indeed, the events there were expected to be the focus of the news-making world.

The convention center was named after a former New York senator, and the honor in that was considerable, because the place is huge—stretching from 34th Street to 38th Street, with 1.8 million square feet of floor space inside. It has hosted many big moments in the thirty years it has been in operation—conventions and performances and trade shows and exhibitions—but none of them would come close to what was supposed to happen in the early morning hours of November 9. Balloons would fall and cheers would ring out and thousands of people would hug and dance and cheer and cry happy tears while fireworks went off on a barge in the Hudson River, which runs right by the site.

But none of it happened. No fireworks, no balloons, no cheering, no dancing. There were tears—a great many tears. But they were not the happy kind. But the most important thing that was supposed to happen that night and didn't is that the person for whom the celebration was being held did not step up to the podium with her husband at her side and thank the people in the hall and the tens of millions watching on TV for electing her president of the United States—the first female president in America's 240-year history.

It was Hillary Rodham Clinton, former secretary of state, former senator from New York, former first lady of the United States, who was expected to be the woman who would achieve that milestone. Throughout the months of the campaign, Clinton, chosen as the presidential nominee of the Democratic Party, had been consistently leading her opponent, real estate developer and Republican party nominee Donald Trump, in most of the public opinion polls. The race was closer than many people thought it would be—Trump had become enormously popular among tens of millions of Americans—but Clinton was still seen as the near-certain winner. On Election Day, the *New York Times* calculated the likelihood of her winning at 91 percent. Princeton University put it even higher—at 99 percent.

But the victory never happened.

States that Clinton fought hard to win—Florida, Ohio, North Carolina—chose Trump instead. States she was expected to win easily—Pennsylvania, Wisconsin, Michigan—she also lost. At 2:00 a.m., her campaign chairman took the stage. Votes were still being counted in many states, and though it looked very likely Clinton would lose, there was still a chance.

"It's been a long night and a long campaign," the chairman said. "But we can wait a little longer, can't we? Everybody should head home. You should get some sleep."

They actually didn't have to wait. Before many of those people could get home, and well before they could fall asleep, the uncertain outcome became certain. Clinton made a phone call to Trump, acknowledging her defeat and congratulating him on his victory. It is a ritual of American election nights: the loser calls the winner. Clinton, who had fully expected to be the person receiving the call, abided by the tradition.

In all elections, of course, there is sorrow among the losers and joy among the winners, and that was true on this night too. Nearly 63 million Americans had gone to the polls and voted for Trump, had expected to be disappointed and instead saw the man they had chosen elevated to the White House. But for the losers, there was a special bitterness in that number. The fact was that even more Americans—65.8 million of them—had voted for Clinton, making her the winner by nearly three million votes.

In the American system, however, that vote, called the popular vote, is not what actually decides who wins the election. What makes the real difference is the particular combination of states each candidate wins. Each state is assigned a certain number of votes, called electoral votes, depending on the size of its population: California, with the biggest population in the nation, gets fifty-five electoral votes. Ohio, the seventh most populous state, gets eighteen. Wyoming, the least populous, gets three. Taken together, there are 538 electoral votes. The candidate who wins 270—or one more than half—becomes president.

Usually, the popular vote winner and the electoral vote winner are the same, but on a few occasions, it's gone the other way, with the person who gets fewer popular votes winning just the right mix of states to reach 270 electoral votes. It happened in 1876 and 2000, which is why no one ever heard of President Samuel Tilden or President Al Gore, even though more people voted for them than the actual presidents, Rutherford B. Hayes and George W. Bush. And it happened again in 2016, which is why no one ever heard of President Hillary Clinton either.

That did not make Trump an illegitimate president. Americans may object to the electoral system we have—and many do—but until that system is changed, the nation accepts the presidents it produces.

But there was something else about Trump's victory that bothered people who were not his supporters—and even some who were. He had run an unusual campaign, a harsh campaign, one in which he said angry and sometimes ugly things. He spoke ill of Mexicans and Muslims. He mocked Senator John McCain—an American hero who suffered more than five years of torture and imprisonment during the Vietnam War. He got into a public argument with the Muslim American parents of an American soldier killed in the Iraq war. And over the course of the campaign, as well as his career, he said things about women that shocked a lot of people.

He criticized the physical appearance of a woman who ran against him for the Republican nomination in the earlier months of the presidential campaign, as well as the appearance of the wife of one of the men who had also run. He retweeted a tweet that referred to newscaster Megyn Kelly as "a bimbo." He had called TV personality Rosie O'Donnell "fat" and entertainer Bette Midler "ugly." During one of his debates with Clinton, he dismissed her as a "nasty woman."

Most troubling was a recording from 2005 that surfaced during the presidential campaign, in which Trump boasted about meeting beautiful women and kissing them without asking. "I just start kissing them," he said. "I don't even wait." Much worse, he also said that he would grab women by the vagina—though he used a vulgar word to describe that body part.

That surely cost him some votes, but most of the people who liked him still liked him. And when the recording was released, he apologized for what he'd said and, on the whole, his supporters forgave him.

Other people, though, didn't forgive him, especially the women who were hoping that, at long last, one of their own would become president. Instead the next president was going to be another man—the forty-fifth in a row—and one who seemed less inclined than most men to take their concerns seriously.

"I think I must be dreaming. I don't think I'm awake," said one woman at the Javits Center that night. "I'm in a fog."

There were ways out of that fog, however. Even though the election was lost, women's commitment to equal rights and equal opportunity was not. Trump had won, but he would not be officially inaugurated and begin his term of office for more than two months, on January 20, 2017, in Washington, D.C. On that day, the streets of Washington would belong to the inaugural parade. The day after, January 21, those same streets—and streets all over the country—would belong to American women and girls.

Hillary Clinton was not the first woman to run for president, even if she was the first with a realistic chance of actually winning. As far back as 1872, almost fifty years before American women were even allowed to vote, a political activist named Victoria Woodhull announced her candidacy for the presidency, campaigning for the rights of Black people, who had been freed from slavery only seven years earlier, as well as for women and laborers.

Woodhull's campaign went nowhere; the Republican Party renominated President Ulysses S. Grant, and the Democratic and Liberal Republican Parties chose newspaper publisher and former congressman Horace Greeley. Grant crushed Greeley, and few people gave Woodhull any thought at all. Over the generations that followed, many women stepped forward and declared their candidacy too. Some were quite serious: Senator Margaret Chase Smith in 1964, Congresswoman

Shirley Chisholm in 1972. For some the run was just for fun. In 1940, radio comedian Gracie Allen announced that she was running for president and that she had founded her own party. Its name? The Surprise Party. The biggest surprise of all was that she actually got 42,000 votes, mostly from fans who wrote in her name on election ballots on which she was not even listed. President Franklin Roosevelt, who was reelected to a third term, received 27 million votes.

It was not until 1984 that the Democratic Party did nominate a woman—but for vice president—choosing New York congresswoman Geraldine Ferraro, who ran with presidential candidate Walter Mondale. In November, Mondale and Ferraro were clobbered by President Ronald Reagan and Vice President George H. W. Bush, who won forty-nine of fifty states. In 2008, the Republican Party also nominated a female vice presidential candidate, selecting Alaska governor Sarah Palin to run on a ticket with Senator John McCain. They lost too, in an election that made Barack Obama the first Black president.

So when Hillary Clinton ran for president *and* was nominated by the Democratic Party *and* was favored to win the election *and* did win the popular vote but still wound up standing to the side and watching a man be inaugurated instead, the pain for many women was keen. It did not help that female voters could not even look to the Congress for solace. There are 435 people in the U.S. House of Representatives, and going into the 2016 election, only 88 of them were women. Of the 100 people in the U.S. Senate, only 20 were women. When the votes were counted on election night, things had not improved much, with the total number of women in Congress creeping up to just 92 in the House and 23 in the Senate. That's 21 percent and 23 percent respectively— far below the 50 percent that would be fair.

It was in Hawaii, which is six hours behind the East Coast time zone, that the long election night of 2016 ended last. The state had overwhelmingly chosen Clinton that day, giving her 62 percent of the vote, which meant an awful lot of sad Hawaiians after the final results were announced.

Among those voters staying up late and brooding over the results was Teresa Shook, a lawyer and teacher from Indiana who had moved to Hawaii after she retired. She was the mother of two and the grandmother—or tutu in the Hawaiian language—of four, and on election night she found herself worrying about her grandchildren. The American fight for women's rights had been going on at least since the delegates to the Seneca Falls Convention gathered in 1848. Now, in 2016, it looked like a significant threshold would be crossed, with a woman at last becoming president. With Clinton's loss—and with her loss to a man who had spoken so badly about women—Shook wondered if today's girls, like the girls of so many previous generations, would still come of age in an unequal world.

Women were accustomed to the idea of an unequal world, of course, and that very familiarity with unfairness was another thing that made Clinton's loss even harder to take. There was a powder-keg quality to the anger and frustration women were feeling that night—the accumulated but too-often unexpressed resentment at the unequal representation in Congress; at the fact that working women, on average, earn less pay than men, even when they're doing the same job as men; at the fact that men in government write laws that can affect the health and the bodies of women, ignoring what those women themselves would choose if they had the same power. The loss of a single presidential election was bad, but the pain and rage tonight were about so much more. The keg of explosive powder had been getting fuller and fuller for centuries. The election of 2016 became the struck match.

Teresa Shook was one of the people who felt the fire. Unable to sleep, she flipped on her computer, logged on to her Facebook page, and began typing out an idea that had been running through her head for much of the evening. She remembered the great marches of the past—for civil rights, for workers' rights, against the Vietnam War—and she thought that a similar march in Washington on January 21 would go a long way toward reminding America that women would continue fighting for their rights.

She didn't type long and she didn't type much; the idea was simple, after all. Then she clicked the post button and waited for a response. There was nothing at first, and then still nothing, and then a single *ping*. A friend had read the post and liked the idea. Another *ping* followed, sent by another friend. Then came another and then a few more—a little pattering of *ping*s like the start of a light rain.

At that, Shook decided that it might be a good idea to start a separate Facebook page exclusively devoted to the plans for a march, just in case more people wanted to be part of it. So she did that and invited forty of her friends to join and a couple dozen of them responded. Then she turned off her computer and climbed into bed, satisfied that she had done her very small bit on a very long day, and she at last fell asleep.

When she woke up, she checked the page again. In just the hours she'd been in bed, the light rain had become a full-blown storm. More than 10,000 people had joined the group overnight and had committed to marching, and another 10,000 had said that they were at least interested. All by herself, it seemed, Shook had started something very big—but in fact, she and her group were not alone.

Around the country, a few other people had had a similar idea and had set up pages of their own. Among them was a New York fashion designer named Mari Lynn Foulger, who went by the marketing name Bob Bland, partly because she liked the idea of mixing up men's and women's names and fashions, making it a little easier for all people to dress as they like. During the election, Bland had done a brisk business selling shirts with NASTY WOMAN printed on the front—taking back the words Trump had used to describe Clinton and hoping to make them not a criticism but a statement of defiance. You may not like a woman who is proudly nasty, but you'd better show her some respect.

Bland was sort of famous and her page got some attention; Shook wasn't the slightest bit famous, but for some reason her page was the one that was attracting the most people. Maybe it was the way she'd phrased her post, maybe it was simply the fact that she was a grandmother who was defying the traditional image of grandmothers as modest. Either way, Bland and Shook decided to combine their efforts, with the grandma taking the lead. Then they gathered in all of the other groups that were calling for a Washington demonstration too.

That was a cooperative strategy that had worked before, when the Southern Christian Leadership Congress, the NAACP, the Congress of Racial Equality and a few other organizations combined their efforts to launch the March on Washington in 1963. As with that march, the women organizing this one needed a name for their demonstration and they at first came up with the "Million Woman March," since it was simple, ambitious and powerful sounding. But the name was not new. In 1997, there had been a Million Woman March in Philadelphia, when hundreds of thousands of Black women gathered to stand up for their rights. To borrow that name now would feel, to some, like stealing it.

The matter of the name was more complicated than that, however, exposing a bigger division among the organizers. The march was being led mostly by white women, which made it a little problematic in the same way the 1848 Seneca Falls women's rights convention was. In both cases, it was Black women—who were oppressed on the basis not only of their gender but also of their race—whose needs and grievances were the greatest. Shouldn't white American women have risen up to help them before, and shouldn't they let them take the lead now? The questions were a little like the ones that get asked when a city cuts its public school budget, providing less money for books and lunches and sports equipment to all schools. The decision affects all the schools in the city—modern, well-equipped ones in wealthier, often whiter communities, as well as the older, poorer ones in less wealthy, often Black communities. There's nothing wrong with white families demonstrating against that, but the Black families might ask, "Where were you before? We've had this problem all along."

And that wasn't the only division in the women's march. In the past, two of the organizers, Tamika Mallory and Carmen Perez, were rumored to have shared an ugly and untrue rumor claiming that Jewish people had been the leaders of the slave trade between Africa and the United States. And Mallory had also been openly supportive of an American Nation of Islam minister named Louis Farrakhan who had expressed all manner of bigotry toward Jews. Calls began going out throughout the women's march for anyone associated with such hateful speech to resign.

The idea that such divisions could occur among so unified a group surprised some organizers, but it shouldn't have. Throughout history, even the best and most powerful uprisings have stumbled, tripped up by the fact that the people who lead them are like any other people—imperfect, argumentative, driven by passions and differing opinions.

The women's march nonetheless pressed on, and the matter of its name became one of the things that helped the organizers overcome their differences. Since they were borrowing the structure of the 1963 March on Washington, they hoped to borrow the name—and honor the name—calling their demonstration the Women's March on Washington. But having learned from their stumble over the name of the Million Woman March, they contacted someone whose blessing they figured they'd need: Bernice King, the youngest child of the Reverend Martin Luther King Jr., who had delivered his landmark "I Have a Dream" speech during the march more than half a century earlier.

Like her father, Bernice King was a minister. And like her father, she saw the power in peaceful demonstration. She readily gave her permission for the name to be used and, at the same time, shared with the women's march organizers an inspirational quote from her mother, Coretta Scott King, who had died in 2006: "Women," Mrs. King had said, "if the soul of the nation is to be saved, I believe you must become its soul."

With that, the march had a date and a place and a name, and with the backing of King, other famous people got involved too, including singers Katy Perry, Ariana Grande, John Legend and Zendaya; actors Scarlett Johansson, Emma Watson and Julia Roberts; and Lin-Manuel Miranda, the composer of *Hamilton*, the musical about the first great uprising in American history—the Revolutionary War. Soon, the 20,000 people who had signed up on Facebook swelled to 100,000, then 200,000 and beyond.

And yet for all that, there was still one thing the march lacked: a universal symbol—something that could mark the women who would take to the streets in the same way that the NASTY WOMAN shirts marked those who wanted to declare their strength even before the election was lost.

It didn't take long before that symbol was born—in a modest shop called the Little Knittery in Los Angeles, California. When the idea for the march was announced, two friends who took classes at the Knittery wanted to make a contribution in some way. They knew that while the weather in Southern California is pleasant in January, it can be bitterly cold in Washington. What anyone who was going to be marching in such conditions needed was a nice knit hat. And since most of the marchers would be female, the hats ought to be pink—the color traditionally associated with femininity. So bright a color would turn up nicely on TV as well, turning all of the participants into one great pink wave. With the help of their knitting instructor, the two women came up with a design for the hat: it would be a more or less the ordinary, head-hugging shape of any knit hat, except it would come to a point at the top on the left and on the right, a bit like the ears of a cat. And it would be called a Pussyhat.

There were a few reasons for the name: For one thing, it rhymes with "pussycat," which is fun and memorable. What's more, the name of the hat would be another opportunity for the women in the march to take back the language. The word "pussy" was the term Trump used for vagina—a way to diminish women, to show them disrespect. Now, as with the adjective "nasty," women would reframe the meaning.

The Little Knittery posted the design of the hat online, and it was quickly downloaded more than 100,000 times. Similar designs were shared on Facebook and other social media sites, and they were downloaded tens of thousands of times too. In San Francisco, stores began reporting that they were running out of pink yarn. The shortage spread to Seattle and then to the Midwest. And there was a very good reason for all of that yarn going into all of those hats: even as Shook's group was still working on organizing the Washington march, plans for sister marches on the same day began popping up too—in New York and Chicago and Los Angeles and Denver and Atlanta and Boston and Philadelphia and Miami; in Helena, Montana, and Austin, Texas, and Park City, Utah; and then, incredibly, in London and Paris and

Tokyo and Stockholm; in Auckland, New Zealand and Beirut, Lebanon, and Bogotá, Colombia, and Nairobi, Kenya. What started as an event in Washington, D.C., was quickly becoming a global phenomenon.

It was more than the soul of the nation that seemed as if it was going to be saved. It was the soul of the world—and women were indeed taking the lead.

When the day at last arrived, women and girls—as well as men and boys—marched in an astonishing 670 cities around the world. They marched in practically all time zones and on every continent, including Antarctica, where an international group of tourists ranging in age from twenty-four to eighty-seven disembarked their ship in Paradise Bay on the Antarctic Peninsula and formed up along a hiking trail to signal their resolve to the rest of the world.

In Yellowknife, Canada, where the temperature was six degrees below zero, people bundled up and turned out. "It's important to be here in solidarity with women around the world," said one marcher. "These issues aren't just happening in the United States."

In Seoul, South Korea, thousands marched in the cold and the snow. "I want my wife and daughter to be respected as much as men are," said Lee Seong-Kwan, a thirty-three-year-old husband and father who was part of the group. Like a lot of the people marching both in the U.S. and around the world, he understood a larger truth: that women's rights are not *only* women's rights. They are human rights. Everyone is diminished—regardless of race, religion, gender or sexual orientation—when anyone experiences oppression or discrimination. That fact is one reason so many white people turned out at civil rights marches, so many Christians fought to save Europe's Jews during the Holocaust, so many heterosexuals participate in gay pride parades.

And it is the same reason too that so many fathers and sons and brothers and husbands marched in 2017 to lift up the mothers and daughters and sisters and wives they love.

In Mexico City, people marched past the Angel of Independence monument, which commemorates Mexican freedom, and offered a reminder to their neighbor to the north. "Love, not hate, makes America great!" they chanted. It was a spin on Trump's campaign slogan, "Make America great again," and a reminder that mistreating women is not a way to achieve anything like greatness.

But it was the United States that was the center of the world that day, with demonstrations in more than 500 cities. In Washington, an estimated 470,000 people showed up, roughly three times the size of the crowd that had attended Trump's inauguration the day before. More than 1 million rides were taken on the city's subway system in the twenty-four-hour period surrounding the march, nearly breaking the ridership record of 1.1 million, set during President Obama's first inauguration in 2009.

In New York City, organizers expected 100,000 people to join the march, which started on Fifth Avenue at 42nd Street and moved north, past Trump Tower, the new president's New York home, at 56th Street. As it turned out, the crowd exceeded 400,000 people.

"I've lived here all my life," said eighty-eight-year-old New Yorker Helen Evarts, who was part of the crowd. "I protested against the Vietnam War and it was nothing like this."

In Chicago, there were at least 250,000 participants—so many that the intended march along Michigan Avenue was canceled and the participants rallied in Grant Park instead. Forty-nine years earlier, during the Democratic Convention, the same thing happened—with Michigan Avenue shut down and demonstrators redirected to the park. But that time it was a fear of violence that closed the road—and that violence indeed came. This time, there was no such ugliness.

"There is no safe way to march," Ann Scholhamer, one of the organizers of the event, announced in the park. "We are just going to sing and dance and make our voices heard here."

In Stanley, Idaho, about half of the entire population of the town turned out, and if the town is home to just 63 people, well, what of it? Half is still half. In Helena, Montana, a third of the little city's 31,000 people marched. In all, experts put the total U.S. participation at 4.3 million people, more than one in every hundred Americans, making it the largest demonstration in the nation's long history.

Of course, a single march on a single day, no matter its size, cannot change a fundamental rule of human society—which is that, across cultures and centuries, women have been accorded fewer rights and powers than men. But every culture and country makes progress in its own steady way, and that was very much true of the U.S. following the events of January 21, 2017.

Less than two years after the march, Americans once again went to the polls—this time to choose candidates for nearly all offices except president. When the voting was done, the number of women in the Senate jumped to 25 and in the House of Representatives to 102—a record high. Four women were elected governors of their states, bringing the national total to nine. Within a few months of the election, five women announced that they would be running for president in 2020. Women's marches were held again in 2018 and again in 2019 and, like the Earth Day parades that have happened every year since 1970, the women's marches will now be annual events too.

Of course, an "annual" anything need not go on forever. There can come a time when the need for something that happens year after year is, at long last, not needed anymore. That is the goal—maybe not a next-year goal, or a year-after goal, but a someday goal—for the women's marches. As women and girls seize their share of the power to shape the world, men and boys are learning to surrender the share that was never rightly theirs. Over time, the competition will become collaboration—and over time, the genders that equally make up humanity will also equally steer humanity.

A medical tent, in the style of a Native American teepee, during the Standing Rock protests.

TWELVE

Dakota Access Uprising
2016–2017

IT WAS NO surprise to the Great Sioux Nation when the black snake once again made its approach. The Sioux dreaded the snake, and they certainly wished they could avoid the snake. But the time had long passed when they would be surprised by the snake.

The prophecy of the black snake had been shadowing the Great Sioux Nation for more than 400 years. It would come, so the original legends said, in the form of a vast poisoning or a spreading sickness, spoiling the land, killing the animals and the people. It would slither, as snakes do, low to the ground, moving anywhere at will and killing what it touched. And when it had done its worst to the surface of the Earth, it would move underground and claim the very heart of the world.

At first the Sioux were strong enough to stand up to the snake—and so were the other Native American tribes living on the continent with them. Across what is now known as North America, there are estimates that there were once as many as 4,000 different indigenous tribes, representing perhaps as many as 18 million people.

They made their homes in the bitter cold of the Arctic north; in the broiling heat of the desert southwest; in the swampy lands of the humid gulf; in the temperate northeast and the rainy northwest and the windy central plains where the land sizzled in the summer and froze in the winter. They traded with other tribes. They fought battles and brokered peace treaties with them too. They tended their land and raised their children, according to their different cultures and legends and languages, and of all of those societies, the Great Sioux Nation was one of the most prosperous and powerful.

Some of the Sioux's strength came from their willingness to join hands and form a single people out of many different people. The Sioux language was actually a mix of three dialects—the Lakota, the Western Dakota and the Eastern Dakota. Within those three language groups were seven different subtribes. They sprawled across what we now think of as six states: North Dakota, South Dakota, Nebraska, Minnesota, Iowa and Michigan. The land was fed by the Missouri River and was rich with good soil and abundant fish and other wildlife. Living peacefully on that plentiful stretch of continent required the seven subtribes to put aside any differences they might have, so in the seventeenth century, they became an alliance, agreeing to be governed by what they called the Seven Council Fires. To the world at large, they were simply the Great Sioux Nation.

Unity inside the Sioux nation meant they could better face the dangers that lay outside—the most menacing of which were the settlers from the east. The settlers had come from across the ocean, occupying the land and establishing their own nation there, which they eventually called the United States of America. They seized their land from the eastern tribes—the Narragansett, the Montaukett, the Mohegan and others—and, having done that, began spreading farther and farther west.

To the Sioux, the settlers seemed like the black snake prophecy fulfilled—coming to take the tribal land and kill them in the process if that was what was required. The white settlers had plenty of tools that helped them in that murderous work. They had guns for one thing; the Native Americans originally fought their wars and hunted their game with bows and arrows and hatchets and spears, and while those were fierce and deadly weapons, they were nothing compared to rifles and pistols, which could be fired from much greater distances and with much more lethal effects. Ultimately, the Native Americans would trade with the settlers and acquire their own arsenal of guns, but not when the Europeans were first expanding across the continent.

Then too there were the deadly tools the Europeans did not even realize they were carrying: the diseases to which they had developed some immunity over the centuries, but which the Native Americans had never encountered and therefore could not survive. The Europeans came ashore invisibly weaponized with smallpox, chicken pox, malaria, influenza, cholera, measles, scarlet fever and more. Once those diseases infected a single Native American, they could sweep through entire tribes, killing up to ninety percent of entire villages of thousands.

There was also European alcohol. Native Americans had learned to make alcoholic drinks, fermented from plum or corn or cactus. The drinks were not terribly strong and were often used exclusively for ceremonial purposes. The Europeans knew how to make much more potent drinks—much higher in alcohol—and introduced them to the Native Americans. But just as with the diseases the settlers brought, the tribes were not accustomed to the drinks the Europeans gave them and many became dependent on them and sick from them, developing an addiction to something that didn't even exist on the continent until the Europeans showed up.

It took a while before the settlers from the eastern part of the country pressed far enough west to disturb the Sioux directly. The first serious clash did not happen until 1854, when a battle broke out between Sioux warriors and American settlers near Fort Laramie, in land that is now part of Wyoming. The fight, which would shape the Sioux and American nations, was over a cow—a stray that belonged to a European settler but that a Lakota Sioux, whose name translated as High Forehead, had found and killed. He had committed a crime and the tribe might have punished him, but the Americans acted first. Twenty-nine soldiers and their commanding officer entered a Sioux settlement uninvited and unannounced, looking for High Forehead. They confronted the chief, Conquering Bear, and demanded the thief be turned over to them. He refused; it was the right of the tribe to discipline its own. A fight ensued in which Conquering Bear was shot and killed. The enraged Sioux killed all thirty Americans in retaliation.

If there was ever going to be a chance for peace between the Americans and the Sioux, it ended with the death of Conquering Bear. The next spring, American general William Harney led a series of attacks on Sioux communities, the first in a place called Ash Hollow, Nebraska, where he killed half of a small tribe of 250 people, including mothers and children—an act of violence that quickly became known as the Harney Massacre. He next drove his troops into South Dakota and attacked the Sioux near the trading post of Fort Pierre, where the Sioux and the Americans did business together, buying and selling furs and crops and other essentials. After Harney's attack, they would trade no more. The fighting continued into Minnesota, North Dakota and Colorado, with American soldiers killing Sioux in clashes that became known as the Battle of Big Mound, the Battle of Killdeer Mountain, the Battle of the Badlands and the Battle of Dead Buffalo Lake. Most notorious was the Wounded Knee Massacre of 1890, in which ninety mostly unarmed Sioux warriors and 200 women and children were killed near Wounded Knee Creek in South Dakota. The Sioux did win some fights, but they lost many more, and no matter what, it was clear that the American soldiers and settlers—with their superior weaponry and their constant flood of new settlers pouring in from the east—would prevail.

In 1868, there was a flicker of hope for the tribe. With both sides weary of the bloodshed, the American settlers and the Sioux signed the Treaty of Fort Laramie, agreed to in the same place their initial battle had been fought, with both sides promising that: "From this day forward, all war between the parties to this agreement shall forever cease." The Sioux agreed to confine their range to a much-reduced stretch of land including parts of North Dakota, South Dakota and Nebraska. In return for the land the Sioux gave up, the settlers promised that the territory they had remaining to them "shall be set aside for the absolute and undisturbed use of the Indians" and that no person, especially the settlers and soldiers, "shall ever be permitted to pass over, settle upon or reside in the territory." And in case there was any doubt about the sincerity of the terms of the treaty, the settlers and the army added a straightforward promise: "The government of the United States desires peace and is hereby pledged to keep it."

The pledge lasted just six years, after which General George Custer led an expedition to search for gold in the sacred Black Hills, and thereafter thousands of miners poured in. While Custer would die in the Battle of Little Bighorn on June 25, 1876, the Lakota would eventually be confined to the Indian reservations. In 1889, the U.S. Congress passed a law breaking the Fort Laramie treaty, shattering the Great Sioux Reservation into five smaller reservations, with nine million acres left over to be sold to American settlers for ranching and farming. And the Sioux were hardly the only tribe suffering at the hands of the settlers. In those same twenty-one years and for four decades beyond, the American army rampaged across the continent, seizing the land of all the other Native American nations, including the Navajo, Osage, Shoshone, Chippewa, Apache, Wyandotte, Ponca,

Goshute and Pawnee. The tribes were forced onto smaller and smaller reservations, with what land they got being regularly snatched back in bits and parcels as the United States expanded and developed, crowding out and impoverishing the people who were there first.

By the 1950s, the millions of Native Americans who had inhabited the continent when the Europeans first arrived had been reduced—by starvation, poverty, war and disease—to fewer than 330,000, scratching out their livings on ever-shrinking patches of land. The Sioux looked out on the Great Plains that were once theirs, where even the comparatively undeveloped land was crisscrossed by blacktop highways, and reflected bitterly that this, surely, was the black snake prophecy come true. But it was only the first part—the part in which the snake takes the surface of the land. The second part, when the snake goes underground and poisons the heart of the Earth, had still not occurred. And then, in 2014, that vision too seemed about to come true.

In the previous decade, fossil fuel companies had begun extracting enormous amounts of oil from an area called the Bakken fields in northwest North Dakota. The oil was usually carried by train across 1,200 or so miles to a storage facility in central Illinois, from which it could be distributed to refineries and consumers. But train transport could be slow—forever disrupted by bad weather or track repairs. And it could be expensive, what with all the labor required to load the oil into tanker cars and then unload it at the Illinois depot. It would be so much easier just to build a long pipeline underground and pump the oil through it.

A Texas company called Energy Transfer Partners (ETP) hoped to build the pipe, and the government in Washington, as well as the local governments in the plains states, generally approved of the idea. The designers had originally planned a route for the pipe that would run by Bismarck, North Dakota, the state's capital and its second-largest city. If the pipeline ruptured, however, it could contaminate the water supply—and that was no imaginary danger. Since 2010, there had been hundreds of leaks and ruptures in oil and gas pipelines across the country. So ETP agreed to reroute the pipeline. It would now run 1,172 miles from the Bakken fields to Illinois and, on the way, pass directly under the Sioux lands known as the Standing Rock Indian Reservation. Its route would take it beneath the Ogallala Aquifer, a freshwater deposit deep underground that had formed more than a million years ago, and had provided the Sioux with water for centuries. It would also cut across at least two dozen Sioux archaeological sites, as well as across Sioux burial sites. For the Sioux, building a pipeline there would be like building one straight through Arlington National Cemetery in Virginia, where hundreds of thousands of American soldiers, as well as two presidents, are buried.

The snake, clearly, was about to burrow. But the Sioux, who might have lost the battle aboveground, were determined not to lose the one below. As they had had to fight since the death of Conquering Bear in 1854, so too would they fight again.

If there was any advantage the Sioux living on the Standing Rock land had over the blunt force of an oil company and the United States itself, it was the slow and poky way the American government moves, especially when it comes to a construction project. The nineteenth-century U.S. Army might have blitzed the Native American tribes with quick strikes on their ancestral lands, but the twenty-first-century Department of the Interior, Department of Energy and Environmental Protection Agency have to go through many approval steps before a single shovel can turn a single scoop of dirt on a construction project as big as the pipeline. In early 2016, more than two years after the plan was first announced, all of those departments were still studying how much damage the project might do to the land, and at the same time were sifting through 33,000 petitions and legal requests from groups opposing the construction, demanding to see all of the documents and permits that would allow it to be built.

The Sioux were among the groups filing those petitions and lawsuits, but like all the other opponents of the pipeline, they had a sense of impending defeat: the lawsuits were steadily being dismissed; the petitions were being pushed aside, and their environmental concerns were being ignored. The government wanted this pipeline built, and while it might go through the motions of hearing all sides, there was little question how it would rule.

On April 1, 2016, a Sioux elder named LaDonna Brave Bull Allard decided it was finally time to act. Allard was the Standing Rock Reservation's historic preservation officer—the person responsible for keeping the story of the Sioux alive—and she had tribal history deep in her blood. In 1863, her great-great-grandmother, Nape Hote Win, who also went by Mary Big Moccasin, lost her life in the Whitestone massacre in North Dakota, a battle with the U.S. Army in which even more Sioux were killed than in the Battle of Wounded Knee.

With the help of a handful of other Standing Rock tribespeople, Allard announced she was establishing a small camp in the northern stretch of the reservation where part of the pipeline would be built. She pronounced it a site of spiritual preservation and cultural resistance— and that's what it was. But it was more too. It was a place where an uprising, if one were to occur, would take shape. If there was one thing the long history of civil demonstrations had taught people who were rallying for their rights, it was that it always helped to have a place to gather and to defend. For the colonists, it was Boston Harbor, where the British wanted to unload their hated tea. For the people of Stonewall, it was their inn and their street in New York City. For Rosa Parks, it was one seat on one bus. Allard, similarly, would give her people a spot where they could stand.

The word quickly went out from Standing Rock that a resistance to the pipeline was forming. It was spread informally among the 300 remaining tribes of the plains, and Allard and the organizers also reached out in more formal ways: contacting newspapers, magazines and TV networks, and connecting via social media and the internet. Over the course of the few weeks that followed, the publicity effort began having an effect—a little. People trickled into Standing Rock first by the handful and then by the dozens and joined the tiny camp Allard had established. But if the media noticed, they didn't show it, and if the government cared, it surely didn't act, allowing the plans for the site to grind slowly ahead. Allard wasn't the only one mobilizing, however.

Before April was out, a teen group known as the One Mind Youth Movement—which had first formed to battle drug use and suicide among Native American youth, brought on by many factors, including the poverty on too many of the reservations—joined the anti-pipeline movement. It was led by a young Sioux woman named Jasilyn Charger, as well as a friend named Joseph White Eyes, who had brought her into the group. They set up a small prayer camp near the pipeline path, practicing ancient Sioux rituals—conducting a morning water ceremony, tending a sacred fire—and, like Allard, making it clear that if the equipment and the people constructing the pipeline came to Standing Rock, they would stand in their way.

Before long, younger Sioux got involved too. In early May, a thirteen-year-old girl named Anna Lee Rain Yellowhammer organized a petition drive along with thirty other children in the tribe, hoping to collect enough signatures to persuade the government to stop the pipeline. They named their organization ReZpect Our Water, with the Z as a nod to the slang shortening of "reservation" to "rez." Yellowhammer composed the text of the petition and addressed it to the U.S. Army Corps of Engineers, the group that would be responsible for overseeing the construction.

"I am writing this letter to stop the Dakota Access Pipeline," she began. "My great-grandparents are originally from Cannon Ball, North Dakota, where the pipeline will cross the Missouri River . . . They raised gardens, chickens and horses. I want to be the voice for my great-grandparents and my community and ask you to stop the building of the Dakota Access Pipeline."

She went on for a few more sentences—describing the risk of a pipeline break and the damage that would be done to the Missouri River if such an accident occurred. She ended with the Sioux words "Mni wiconi," or *Water is life*.

They were simple words, but they were powerful ones, and they motivated people to act. Within days, more than 80,000 people had signed the petition online, helped in no small part by a video Yellowhammer and her friends released along with it. That caught the attention not just of ordinary people who cared about the Sioux, but of celebrities, who cared too but whose opinion and endorsement could change a lot of minds. Less than three months before, actor Leonardo DiCaprio had won Hollywood's Best Actor Oscar for the movie *The Revenant*, set in the American frontier of the 1820s. He learned of what Yellowhammer was doing and he responded, as so many people do in the twenty-first century and as the great activists of earlier generations could not have imagined, over Twitter, where he had 19 million followers.

"Standing w/ the Great Sioux Nation to protect their water & lands," he wrote. "Take a stand." He added the link to the petition; before long there were more than 140,000 signatories.

Now the Standing Rock protest became a true movement.

Yellowhammer and her group decided that rather than sending their petition to Washington by traditional mail or email, they could bring it by hand, embracing the old tradition of the Sioux who would carry messages great distances by running relays, with each messenger covering a portion of the route and then passing the message on to the next, and on and on till the information had been delivered. In the case of the pipeline, the young Sioux would not simply be carrying their message across tribal lands, but across the full stretch of continent from North Dakota to Washington, D.C.—2,000 miles.

When the runners set out, carrying signs like WATER PROTECTOR and WATER IS SACRED, the media covered that story too. More celebrities were then drawn into the fight: music stars Katy Perry and Zendaya, actors Shailene Woodley and Lupita Nyong'o. Senator Bernie Sanders, who was running for the Democratic Party's presidential nomination, endorsed the cause as well. Solidarity marches were planned in Seattle and Denver. Nineteen cities passed resolutions backing the Sioux and opposing the pipeline.

"Showdown over oil pipeline becomes a national movement for Native Americans," wrote the *Washington Post* as the groundswell grew. The paper quoted one of those Native Americans, forty-eight-year-old Frank White Bull, a member of the Standing Rock tribal council, who was moved by the coming together of the tribes he was seeing on his lands. "You think no one is going to help," White Bull said. "But the people have shown they're here to help us. We made our stance and the Indian Nation heard us. It's making us wanyi oyate—one nation."

The construction company and the policymakers who wanted the pipeline built, however, were not moved by the wanyi oyate, any more than they were by the endorsement of celebrities or by a group of children running a petition from North Dakota to Washington. In late July, the Corps of Engineers issued a 1,261-page report approving of the construction of the pipeline. "I have evaluated the anticipated environmental, economic, cultural and social effects," said one Corps official who granted the final clearance. He concluded that the pipeline was "not injurious to the public interest."

Even then the Standing Rock Sioux wouldn't move, maintaining their position on their land throughout the remainder of July. What's more, their numbers grew, as members of other tribes arrived to stand with them in the common mission of defending Native American lands. In August, Yellowhammer and her runners were scheduled to arrive in Washington, and the Sioux hoped that the petition might have some effect there—though when they did arrive, the government still showed no sign of relenting.

Finally, on September 3, five weeks after the Corps gave its approval, the pipeline construction teams hit back. As the protesters stood at their posts at the camp, three bulldozers rumbled over a ridge and onto the site where the pipeline work was set to begin. They lowered their plows and began gouging a 150-foot-wide trench through the tribal land. The protesters broke toward the bulldozers, but as they did, a helicopter hovered into view overhead and a small fleet of pickup trucks arrived, carrying security guards and trained bite dogs.

In a terrible historical echo of the attack-dog tactics unleashed on unarmed Black people demonstrating for civil rights in the streets of Birmingham, Alabama, in 1963, the guards and the dogs leapt out of their trucks and charged the protesters, who at first scattered but then regrouped. The dogs lunged and growled at the end of their leashes, biting protesters who drew too close and coming away with blood on their snouts. The guards carried a powerful form of pepper spray and fired it into the eyes of the Sioux, who fell away in pain. Other Sioux gathered them up and began rinsing their eyes with water.

"We're not leaving! We're not leaving!" the crowd began to chant as Sioux protesters on horseback wove among them. The horses leapt and frisked nervously at the noise and the violence.

The guards now advanced again, and the dogs, trained to attack, trained to bite, did what their handlers told them. The larger group of Sioux and the smaller group of guards faced off and advanced on each other. The protesters' chant now grew louder, angrier, the "We're not leaving!" replaced by a furious "Get the f— out of here!" It was what can happen when a crowd grows enraged. The guards, greatly outnumbered, sensing the change, began hauling in their dogs and backing toward their trucks. They jumped inside, slammed the doors and scattered fast as the bulldozers retreated too. The protesters, for the moment, had won.

That victory strengthened the resolve of the Standing Rock Sioux and almost without having to say so among themselves, they understood they were now digging in for what would be a long and surely bitterly cold winter, with temperatures on the plains regularly falling well below zero. For the remainder of September and much of October, another lull settled in, with both sides—perhaps frightened by the violence that had already unfolded—allowing the conflict to continue to be fought out in the courts and the government agencies.

On the evening of October 26, however, a rumor began spreading around the camp that the sheriff of Morton County and sheriffs from surrounding counties had ordered the police to attack the next day to disperse the camp. The rumor turned out to be true. Mobilization of police officers throughout the area had been observed. A cold dread settled over the camp. Lynda Mapes and Ellen Banner, a reporter and photographer with the *Seattle Times*, spent the night with the tribe and reported the next day that some of the Sioux had been singing traditional tribal death songs—verses of farewell to be sung when war or other danger looms the next day.

"The land is beautiful," one of the songs begins. "O Sun, now for the last time, come and greet me again."

As it turned out, there would be no Sioux deaths the next day, but there would be violence and injury and reason to fear that death was near. The Sioux, this time, were vastly outnumbered—even with the reinforcements from the other tribes—and the police attacked not just with dogs and handheld pepper spray, but with clubs and concussion grenades—designed to startle and disorient with their sound—as well as with Tasers, which can paralyze with electricity. Guns that fire painful beanbags were used against the protesters as well. Five armored personnel carriers—powerful military vehicles designed to transport soldiers—were also deployed, advancing steadily on the protesters. The bodies of the Sioux would be no match for the power of the machines, and the danger mounted until one tribal elder stepped forward and placed himself between the vehicles and the people.

"Go home," he told the tribe calmly. "We're here to fight the pipeline, not these people." The tribe and activists retreated, but not before 142 of them were arrested.

The standoff and the violence spilled into November, with the police returning, and this time adding rubber bullets to the concussion grenades and the stinging spray. In another echo of Birmingham, they also turned fire hoses on the protesters, though in North Dakota, unlike in Alabama, it was now twenty-three degrees Fahrenheit—well below freezing.

"They're actually trying to hurt people," said one Sioux leader. They succeeded. An estimated 200 Native Americans suffered injuries and a dozen were transported to hospitals.

Yet still the people stayed, still the Sioux stood, even as the temperature dropped and the long winter loomed. Then, finally, on December 4, came a sudden, stunning victory. The Army Corps of Engineers, recognizing that it was still possible to build the pipeline—a little more expensively perhaps, a little more slowly—if it detoured around the Sioux land, announced that the tribe had won, the pipeline would bypass them. It was four months after Yellowhammer and her young runners had arrived in Washington with their petition, and the person to whom it had been delivered was Jo-Ellen Darcy, the Corps' assistant secretary for civil works. She was the person who issued the statement that day.

"The best way to complete the work responsibly and expeditiously," she said, "is to explore alternative routes for the pipeline crossing."

The news rang through the camp. There was cheering and hugging and celebrating. Chants of "Mni wiconi!" broke out everywhere.

"You all did that!" said one tribal leader to the assembled Sioux and other tribespeople. "Your presence has brought the attention of the world!" Then he gave his people news that was better still. "It's time now that we move forward. We don't have to stand and endure this hard winter. We can spend the winter with our families."

Slowly, tearfully, joyously, the victorious Sioux began breaking camp. After eight long months, they would return to their homes— their lands and their waters secured. That, at least, was what they believed. But the black snake had other ways.

It is a singular feature of the United States Constitution that the president of the United States is the commander in chief of the armed forces, including its peacetime operations, like the construction work done by the Corps of Engineers. When the Corps' ruling came down on December 4, Barack Obama was president of the United States, and he accepted it. But forty-seven days later, on January 20, 2017, Donald Trump, who had been elected president early in November, was inaugurated. Four days after the inauguration, in one of his first official acts, he overturned the December 4 ruling.

"The regulatory process in this country has become a tangled-up mess," he said. "This is about streamlining the incredibly cumbersome, long, horrible permitting process." He then signed the executive order with a black Sharpie pen and, with that, the work of the eight months was undone.

There would be more court battles and more petitions filed, and the Sioux and others would fight on. But lawsuits move far more slowly than bulldozers, and construction began almost immediately after Trump's order. By April the pipeline was largely complete, and by June 1, 2017, it began delivering oil.

"I just closed my eyes and said, 'Do it,'" Trump boasted in a speech later that month. "It's up, it's running, it's beautiful, it's great, the sun is shining, the water's still clean."

The Sioux, however, cannot close their eyes. And while the sun will surely keep shining, the water will remain clean only as long as the pipeline never leaks. If it does—when it does, many people fear—the tribal lands and the tribe itself be dealt another blow.

The lessons in that for the Sioux are lessons also for women and Black people and gays and lesbians and transgender people and defenders of the environment and protesters against wars and for the American colonists themselves—for anyone, in fact, who has ever risen up against what was wrong and demanded what is right. There are victories in those battles and there are setbacks—and there is even violence and loss of life. What's enduring, unchanging—a fixed moral star—is the principle of justice. We are a nation and a species that has always followed it and, when necessary, always fought for it.

A NOTE ON SOURCES

HISTORY HAS BEEN recorded by uncounted numbers of people and stored and published in uncounted ways across the generations. In telling the tales of a dozen of America's most significant stories of social and political activism, stretching from 1773 to 2017, I called on many such sources.

The internet, of course, makes historical research vastly easier than it once was, with effectively all of the recorded information in the world available from a fixed spot on a single screen. Work that would have required visiting libraries and universities in multiple countries and cities can be conducted—or at least begun—in a day.

It is the nature of search engines and algorithms that Wikipedia comes up at or near the top of nearly any inquiry. And it is the nature of researchers and students to want to take advantage of that fact. There was a time when Wikipedia was a poor, unreliable source of information, and most teachers, professors and news organizations still forbid or discourage its use. But taking advantage of Wikipedia as a beginning source, especially for an unfamiliar topic, can be helpful. I have found that it offers a general overview of a historical event or an entire field, but no more; it should not be the sole or even a principal source.

Rather, it can point you in directions that will lead you to deeper and more reliable sources.

Newspapers and magazines are often the very best of those sources. Journalism, it is said, is the first draft of history and I have found that to be true. *Time* magazine's near century of publishing provides a rich trove of data going back to its first issue in 1923, all of which is searchable on its website, under the heading "Vault."

The *New York Times*'s archival site, known as TimesMachine, offers an extraordinary vein of historical information too, going back to 1851. The site is available online, though only to subscribers. A less-thorough article archives is available to anyone. In some ways, both of these sources are better than *Time*'s archives, because the *New York Times* is a daily publication, not a weekly. The TimesMachine's disadvantage is that for now, it stops at 2002. For the women's march and Dakota Access Pipeline chapters in *Raise Your Voice,* therefore, the *Times* offered no help.

Local newspapers are exceedingly valuable sources as well—the *Washington Post* for the March on Washington chapter, for example; the *Chicago Tribune* for the chapter on the Democratic Convention. They are typically much more familiar with their communities than national news sources could ever be.

Government records, most of which are searchable online, can be indispensable. The records from the U.S. Centers for Disease Control and Prevention provided important statistics about HIV and AIDS infections when I was researching the ACT UP movement. The U.S. Census provided Native American population numbers in the Dakota Access Pipeline chapter.

Activist and special interest groups are valuable sources for research involving their areas of expertise: the Environmental Protection Agency and the Environmental Defense Fund for environmental research; the

Bulletin of the Atomic Scientists for studies of nuclear power; Lambda Legal, GLAAD, GLESN and others for gay and lesbian rights.

And, of course, when your search points you to a book, read it—or at least the relevant parts. *Triangle: The Fire That Changed America*, by my former *Time* magazine colleague David von Drehle, might be the best book available on the disaster and how it shaped American labor. *Rosa Parks: My Story*, by Ms. Parks herself, is of course the most authoritative source on her life and legacy. And there are a great many books about the Stonewall riots and the Boston Tea Party.

With the aid of the internet, it is also possible—and easy in fact—to watch newscasts or hear radio broadcasts of significant events. Online museums also allow you to browse artifacts and original documents; the National Women's History online museum, for example, or the Smithsonian Institute's National Museum of African American History and Culture offer wonderful online resources.

Ultimately, every research project is a journey, with informational detours and tributaries taking you places and teaching you things that you never imagined. Follow where the research leads, even if it's to sources you don't wind up using in your work. You will be better and wiser for taking the time and doing the learning.

INDEX

Page numbers in *italics* refer to illustrations.